THE HISTORIC LICKING COUNTY JAIL

Untold Stories of the Murderers Who Lived There

by Neil D. Phelps

To Sil

Neil Phelps

8-5-2017

All photos were taken by the author, if not otherwise indicated.

Published by Neil D. Phelps, Granville, Ohio 43023
Produced with support by PhoenixGraphix.us
Printed by CreateSpace.com

ISBN 978-0-9889971-6-5

Contents

Acknowledgments 2

Introduction 3

1. History of the Jail 4

2. Jail Escapes 19

3. The Lynching of Carl Etherington 23

4. Suicides in the Jail 30

5. Jail Damage 42

6. Murderers of Licking County 45

7. Paranormal Activity at the Jail 86

8. Anonymous Interviews 92

9. Closing of the Jail 95

10. Other Jails of Licking County 98

11. Sheriffs of Licking County 99

Notes 101

References 102

About the Author 105

Acknowledgments

Much of the information in this book I acquired with the help of Bill Markley of the Licking County Records and Archives Department; Emily Larsen and Jennifer Lusetti, of Licking County Historical Society; Kevin Bennett and E. Chris Evans, Licking County historians; Teri Long and Andréa Vantu of Newark, Ohio; and the Licking County Public Library, Newark, Ohio. I especially want to thank my editors, Eleanor Hicks of Granville, Ohio, and Wendy Hollinger, owner of Phoenix Graphix Publishing Services, Granville, Ohio, and her staff; the Licking County Commissioner's Journal; and the newspaperarchive.com website, which provided valuable historic information about the jail, and the many inmates who served time here.

Introduction

The Licking County jail was completed in 1889, and served the county for 98 years. The previous jail was built in 1840 but condemned in 1887 due to inadequate ventilation, a lack of provisions to separate the men from the women, and concerns that it was not secure enough to house more hardened criminals. Much of the history of the jail, including murders and suicides that took place, will be discussed. Although this jail has a rich history, not all of it is something to be proud of; however, times were different then. Some things that were once commonplace would be unthinkable today. The history of the jail, information about the inmates, and references to sources has been documented as accurately as possible.

Licking County Historic Jail, Newark, Ohio

History of the Jail

It has been decades since the last inmate walked out of the old Licking County jail. What remains is a history waiting to be told: a history of the nearly one hundred years the jail was in operation, and the inmates who served time there.

The Licking County Historic Jail is located at Third and Canal Street, just south of the Licking County Courthouse in downtown Newark, Ohio. It is one of the oldest and most interesting structures in Licking County, and possibly in Ohio. Within its walls are volumes of history waiting to be told, history that began on June 12, 1888 when the county commissioners purchased the P. Smith & Sons Lumber Company for $11,000. This would become the site of the new jail. Soon, an announcement was made that bids for the building of the jail would be received in forty days.

Sheriff Andrew Crilly. *Courtesy of the Licking County Historical Society.*

A committee was appointed by the Common Pleas Court to review plans and specifications for the new jail. The committee included the county commissioners; Probate Judge Reese; Mr. Lennox, the Licking County clerk; Mr. Wilford Smith, a private citizen; and Sheriff Andrew Crilly. Crilly became Licking County's twenty-third sheriff in 1887, and the first to live in the sheriff's quarters of the new jail. He remained sheriff until 1893, and was later elected Justice of the Peace until 1903. [1]

The J.W. Yost Company, an architectural firm from Columbus, Ohio, was selected to draw up plans and specifications for the new jail. Joseph W. Yost was a well-known architect who also designed the Horton Building on the Ohio State Campus, and a prison of similar architecture in Woods County Ohio, near Bowling Green.

Born in Clarington, Ohio in 1847, Yost began his architectural studies in 1869 under the direction of Joseph Fairfax of Wheeling,

Joseph W. Yost, architect. *Courtesy of the Licking County Historical Society.*

West Virginia. During his career, which included a partnership with Columbus-based Frank Packard, Yost designed around 230 buildings, including several courthouses, public buildings, and institutions in both Ohio and West Virginia.

Following the selection of Yost, the committee began receiving bids for the building of the jail and sheriff's residence. A bid of $68,685 was accepted from the well-known and highly respected Hibbert and Schaus Construction Company, also in Columbus.

Shortly before construction began, a change in plans was already being discussed. The Board of Commissioners met in a joint session on August 22, 1888, to consider building the new jail and sheriff's residence out of brown sandstone instead of red pressed brick, as originally called for in the contract. The change in the contract also called for Bedford limestone to be used in all the trimmings, which is evident around the windows and the pillars at the front entrance. An agreement was signed by all parties involved on September 15,

1888. The Board of Commissioners agreed to pay an additional $9,475 to the Hibbert and Schaus Construction Company, and soon sandstone blocks were being quarried from Millersburg, Ohio. [2]

On May 7, 1889, Hibbert and Schaus presented a proposal for erecting cells for female inmates on the fourth story of the jail, something that had been overlooked in the original contract. This was important, as one of the reasons for building a new jail was to provide separate housing for male and female inmates, something the previous jail had lacked.

Hibbert and Schaus stated that they would furnish all necessary materials, and erect and complete the cells and ceiling for the fourth story, according to the plans furnished by J. W. Yost, for the sum of $7,700. This would be in addition to the original bid of $68,685 and the $9,475 paid to cover the cost of changing building materials. [3]

"A Splendid Building Rapidly Nearing Completion" was the headline in the *Newark Weekly Advocate* on May 15, 1889, when it reported that two stories of the building were already complete.

Construction on the jail was moving at a rapid pace, but it was becoming clear that there were going to be some serious cost overruns. This was largely due to changing the contract from brick to sandstone, and erecting cells on the fourth floor which had not been included in the original contract. The cost of shipping the sandstone blocks from Millersburg could have been minimized by transporting them by freight wagons thirty miles to New Philadelphia. There, they could have been loaded onto a canal boat and brought to Newark. Canal boats were towed by horses or mules at a speed of approximately four miles per hour. This would have been about a 73-mile trip by canal boat and would have taken a considerable amount of time, so the sandstone blocks were shipped primarily by train instead, resulting in a greater expense.

In November of 1889, after roughly eighteen months of construction, the new jail was finished. Following its completion, an invitation was extended to the public to come and visit the new building before it began its formal operations.

"We feel justified in saying that Licking County now has one of the best, and most substantial jails in the state; one [of] which the taxpayers of the county may justly be proud" said one of the county commissioners. [4] The new jail was indeed an impressive sight. Four stories high, with several small turrets, it also had impressive artistic features. Unique carvings decorated the windows and small animal sculptures—including a snake, a cat, and a frog that collected rainwater in its mouth— peered down from the walls. The jail also had comfortable living quarters for the sheriff, with spacious rooms and beautiful stained glass windows.

Not everyone was pleased with the new jail, however. It had run significantly over budget, at a total cost of $120,000. Many taxpayers were extremely upset that the final cost was nearly double the original bid, especially because it was not just the change in building materials and construction of the fourth-floor cells that had added to the cost. It was discovered that the county commissioners had visited a Toledo company and spent $1,716.10 on furniture for the sheriff's quarters, without advertising for a bid. When Mr. G. Scott, who ran one of the largest furniture houses in central Ohio, was asked what his cost would have been, he said he could duplicate the order for $800 with the same or better furniture. This would have been less than half the price paid to the Toledo company. [5]

It was also noted that when the furniture reached Newark, the same truck containing the furniture for the jail also contained seven pieces of expensive furniture addressed to two of the county commissioners, and to the mother-in-law of one of them. Perhaps this was just an oversight, or an honest error in shipping instructions, but such a case would have been highly unlikely. No further discussion was ever made about this matter, but public discontent about the jail's cost can be seen in the following editorial from *The Newark*

Carvings on the exterior of the jail included a snake, cat and frog.

American, dated December 5, 1889: [6]

"That the taxpayers should have been forced to pay one hundred thousand dollars or more for a Children's Home, in which to support less than a hundred of God's unfortunate is beyond question, a shame and outrage. And yet, it is a fact that that amount was expended on a jail and its furnishings. That much money would have been enough to erect a handsome one thousand-dollar house for each of the children in that institution. Someone was to blame for this fraud and outrage and it would be well for our people to search out the responsible parties and seek a remedy against such outrages in the future." [7]

In spite of the cost overruns and complaints from some taxpaying citizens, the jail was now complete and Sheriff Crilly moved into his new living quarters.

Once he was settled in, it became common for him to entertain the judge and members of the jury in the residence of the jail. At 7:30 the guests would arrive and after a short social time, supper was announced. After a luxurious meal, the remainder of the evening was spent playing games and partaking in social conversation. Of course, this practice would not be acceptable today, especially as these dinners quite possibly took place on the taxpayers' dime. Sheriff Crilly understandably did not extend this generosity to the jail's inmates; instead, he implemented strict standards for the prisoners, including rigid rules for visiting hours, and when lawyers and clergy members were allowed in the jail.

With its impressive tower-like structures peering over the fourth story, the jail seems to beg you to come inside for a closer look. But don't be fooled; once inside it becomes obvious that, outside of the sheriff's quarters, this is not a place you would want to call home.

Jail cell.

The jail was built to house up to 126 inmates, with each 8'x 8' cell holding four prisoners, although when space was limited, as many as six prisoners might be crowded into a cell. These conditions would certainly not be allowed to exist today, but at the time it was not uncommon for prisoners to endure cramped and overcrowded conditions.

Each cell block contained eight cells, with male inmates taking up the first three floors, and female inmates residing on the fourth. The cell doors could be individually unlocked by turning one of the hand-wheels protruding from the wall on the outside of the cell block. These hand-wheels were sometimes referred to as "knuckle busters" because you could easily scrape your knuckles on the cement wall while turning the wheel.

A catwalk around each of the first three floors allowed the deputies to patrol the cells in view of the inmates. Viewports installed at the end of the catwalks enabled the deputies to look through to the other end from outside the jail cell area. These ports could also be used as gun ports, allowing deputies to aim their guns through the opening in the wall, should the need arise. It is not known if the ports were ever used this way, however.

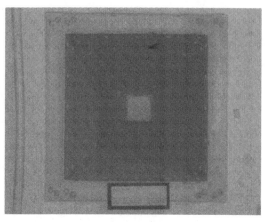

Viewport/gunport, as seen from inside the cell block.

Each of the four cell blocks contained a bathing area, consisting of a small enclosure with a bathtub placed on the cement floor over a drain pipe. This area was secured by a large steel barred door that was closed and locked behind the inmates. Water was brought in by buckets, heated on a stove, and poured into the bathtub. Not everyone would get a fresh tub of water, though. Only the first

Visiting booth.

inmate was fortunate enough to enjoy the luxury of bathing in a fresh tub of heated water. The bath water would then be shared with other inmates.

Bathing and a change of clothes were available just once a week. Sometime during the 1920s, when running water became available, shower stalls (shown at right) were installed on each floor of the jail, replacing the bathtubs.

The jail also contained a chapel where services were held each Sunday from 1:30 to 4:00 p.m., and a visiting booth, where friends and

Shower stall. *Courtesy of Jessica Phelps.*

13

Jail chapel. *Courtesy of Virginia Beach.*

relatives could converse with inmates through a secure opening; the names of some inmates are still visible on the walls of the visiting booth today. There was also a disciplinary cell, and a larger cell known as the Dungeon.

Located in the basement of the jail, near the chapel, the Dungeon was possibly used for temporary confinement of the drunk and disorderly, as well as solitary confinement for troublesome inmates, before being converted to an intake cell. Once new prisoners were fingerprinted and processed in, they would be assigned to a cell, while their personal belongings were stored in the property room next to the intake cell. The name of each prisoner, along with the crime they committed, the number of days they spent in the jail, and any time they may have spent in the Dungeon, was recorded in the jail registers. These jail registers are a significant and important part of the jail's history and are maintained and stored at the Licking County Records & Archives Department.

The Dungeon.

According to a retired deputy, the disciplinary chamber was located on the first or second floor, and consisted of a small compartment large enough for an individual to get inside, but not tall enough to allow for standing. Inmates sent to the chamber were thus forced to remain in an uncomfortable crouched position, sometimes for several hours. This method of discipline was often used to punish inmates who caused severe damage to their cells— such as breaking a sink or destroying a mattress— and is believed to have been in use into the 1950s.

In 1906, the Board of Licking County Visitors—a committee that periodically inspected Licking County buildings for cleanliness and adherence to general operating procedures—visited the jail and recorded the following conditions:

Baths and a change of clothing provided once per week.

Bedding changed once per month.

Kind of beds: canvas hammocks

Jail registers.

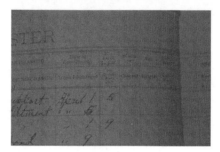

One chair and a night bucket in each cell.

Gas lights.

Heat provided by coal; later, by a hot air furnace.

These conditions were considered normal at that time.

When the jail was inspected on December 10, 1915, the Board reported that there were nine prisoners on the first floor, nine on the second, and seven on the third. They also reported that sanitary conditions were not the best. The report stated that some gas jets used for lighting in the jail had broken mantels, causing high flames and excessive fumes. The gas jets with broken mantels were often used to heat water for the prisoners so they could wash their clothes, which did not help the problem. The recommendation was made to use a stove for heating water instead, thereby avoiding much smoke, dust, and hazardous fumes. It was also recommended that more attention be given to ventilation, although this last suggestion may have seemed unnecessary; most of the windows in the men's cellblocks were open, even in the winter, as the large coal furnace often made the jail uncomfortably warm. One employee attempted to justify the present condition of the jail by stating that the county commissioners would not furnish brooms and other equipment necessary to keep the jail clean, but the commissioners denied refusing any request to purchase cleaning supplies. [8b]

On September 20, 1917, the Board of Visitors reported a total of 30 prisoners. It was then recommended that electric lights be installed, as the present system was inadequate to light the building when the gas pressure was low. A recommendation was also made to install plumbing to improve the sanitary conditions. These recommendations were carried out, along with the installation of an elevator.[i] This elevator has been out of operation since the jail was closed in 1987; however, with the money raised through fundraisers and donations, it may be possible for it to be repaired and re-certified. This would allow individuals with limited mobility to see and enjoy the entire jail, instead of just the first floor.

Serious Overcrowding Reported

The Licking County jail was designed to house a maximum of 126 inmates under normal conditions, but may have housed as many as 165 inmates at times. Reports by the Board of Licking County Visitors do not indicate that severe overcrowding was a common problem, at least not during the inspections conducted in 1915 and 1917. However, during the early 1970s there were times when as many as six male prisoners were squeezed into cells intended for a maximum of four inmates. One person would occupy each of the four bunks, while the other two would sleep under the bottom bunks on each side of the cell. This small space would make it difficult or impossible to turn over. [8a]

Even without the problem of overcrowding, the note shown on the following page, found on the wall in one of the cells, probably conveys the true feelings of many inmates who served time in this jail.

Photo courtesy of Eric Glosser.

Jail Escapes

There has probably never been a jail built that someone wasn't able to break out of and the Licking County jail, although one of the most secure jails of its time, was no exception. One of the first successful escapes occurred in March of 1895, when Sheriff John Chilcote was

absent. Four prisoners broke out of jail, two of whom left for parts unknown. The other two were found enjoying a square meal in the sheriff's private dining room, and promptly escorted back to their cells.

Six months later, Sheriff Chilcote left for a trip to Kansas, leaving Sim Priest, the jailer, in charge. When Priest noticed that the cell occupied by prisoner James Costley was filthy, he had it scrubbed down. The cot, however, was in such bad shape that he had it burned. Later that evening Priest took another bed to Costley. After setting it up, Priest remarked that he would lock the cell as soon as he finished making the bed.

Sheriff John Chilcote. *Courtesy of the Licking County Historical Society.*

Priest went away to take care of other business, but forgot to lock the door, allowing Costley the opportunity to roam about the jail at will. Costley walked out of his cell, and gained access to the outside of the corridor where he was able to unlock the other seven cell doors, leaving nine prisoners at liberty to escape. Three inmates stayed in their cells, while the other six waited on the south side of the corridor until the jailer turned out the lights, and then made their escape. Two were later recaptured, but the remaining four successfully got away.

After two successful escapes within six months, a citizen made the comment that "if Sheriff Chilcote absents himself from the city two or three more times when his presence is needed here in Licking County, we will have no further use for a jail." [9] At that time, the Licking County jail was one of the strongest and best constructed jails in the country. How prisoners confined in it could so frequently effect their escape, seemingly with little difficulty, was a mystery to the public.

Seventeen-year-old Boy Outwits Jailer

On February 25, 1896, while Sheriff Chilcote was still in office, another inmate escaped from jail. This time it was a young boy who outwitted the jailer and escaped from his second-floor cell. Wilbur McCormick, age 17, was awaiting examination by a grand jury on the charge of burglarizing the R. M. Davidson's Cigar Factory and stealing 28 boxes of cigars with his friend, Henry Siegel.

After hearing about prisoners escaping from jail, McCormick decided to test his skills. He obtained an iron rod that he used to break the lock on his cell door, giving him access to the corridor surrounding the jail cells. When Flavius Haslett, the jailer, started up the stairs with the boy's breakfast, young McCormick heard him coming and hid in the corridor. When Haslett entered the cell, the boy came around the corridor and slammed the door, locking the jailer in.

McCormick then made his way to the cellar and escaped through an unbarred window. After getting free, he went to his home on North Fourth Street where he was seen by his father, who advised him to return to the jail, give himself up, and let the law take its course. The boy, however, did not see it that way; after bidding his father good-bye he disappeared, never to be heard from again.

It was about half an hour after McCormick's escape that the jailer's cries for help were finally heard and he was set free. In spite of the sheriff's efforts to keep this embarrassing story quiet, it was soon discovered by the media and printed. [10]

Two Prisoners Escape in Broad Daylight

Another escape occurred in 1907, while Smith L. Redman was sheriff. Three men had already been making their plans to escape from the county jail; all they needed to do was wait for the right opportunity. Occasionally, prisoners would be given access to the corridor outside the jail cells for the purpose of exercise. During one of these occasions, the three men were able to overtake a guard and a trustee, pushing both of them into one of the cells and locking the door as it slammed shut. The prisoners then made their way up the steps to the fourth floor, where they opened a window and climbed down using some sheets they had tied together. The first two men— William Rogers, age 25, who was charged with larceny, and Stanley Weslek, age 26, who was being held for burglary— made their escape in plain view of several people passing by in the street below. The third prisoner began to descend from the window, but climbed back in and returned to his cell when he heard the alarm sounding.

Neither Rogers nor Weslek were ever heard from again, and it is not known if the third man received extra time for attempting to escape. This illustrates once again that a prisoner who was able to escape and make his way out of town was unlikely to be caught, as there was virtually no reliable means of tracking people during that time period. [11]

Rewarded for Good Behavior

At times, an inmate might be allowed access to the catwalk or corridor for good behavior. This was the case with Milton Solomon, a federal prisoner being held in the Licking County jail by Sheriff Elijah Bryan, on charges of auto theft and white slavery (running a prostitution ring). On November 10, 1921, Solomon was given the privilege of access to the catwalk. When Tom Bucy, the jailer, entered the cell block and turned to lock the door, Solomon hit him over the head, knocking him unconscious. Solomon then ran to the cellar, crawled through an unbarred window, and escaped. Two years later, he was captured in New Jersey and sent to the Atlanta Federal Penitentiary for crimes he had committed in that state. After being incarcerated there for about one week, he committed suicide on January 30, 1923. He used his bed sheet suspended from a steel girder over his cell, tying one end around his neck and jumping from his cot.

Carl Etherington. *Courtesy of the Licking County Historical Society.*

The Lynching of Carl Etherington

In the early 1900s, many Midwestern states were fighting between those who wanted to be able to buy and sell alcohol, and those who supported the Temperance Movement. This fight was especially heated in Ohio, as the Temperance Movement, the Anti-Saloon League, and the Christian Temperance Union all had their headquarters near Westerville.

In 1908, the Ohio General Assembly passed the Rose County Local Option Act. This was a result of legislation proposed by Ohio Senator Isaiah Rose, which empowered counties to hold local option elections. The law allowed each county to vote on whether they wanted to be wet or dry. In a vote held on December 7, 1908,

23

William Howard. *Courtesy of the Licking County Historical Society.*

Licking County residents voted to go dry by a majority of 745 votes. However, the city of Newark overwhelmingly voted to be wet. Just a few weeks after the vote, the Licking County option election was contested and a petition was filed in probate court by George H. Fromholtz representing the liquor interests. Fromholtz charged that the voting on December 7 should be null and void because the petition upon which the election was based and held was not signed by 35 percent of the votes cast in Licking County, as required by law. However, in spite of the contested results, the votes stood.

Alcohol was very important to Newark's economy at that time. The American Bottle Company had a beer bottle factory in Newark that employed about 2,000 people, and there were 80 saloons in town, 54 of them in the downtown area alone. The local pubs were social places, and drinking was part of the culture. The Rose Law was a point of contention because the people of Newark voted to stay wet. This was a large part of what led to a most tragic event in Newark's history.

On July 8, 1910, Carl Etherington, a young deputized detective, arrived in Newark from Cleveland. Etherington was part of a group of detectives hired by the National Anti-Saloon League to shut down illegal bars during an early attempt at prohibition. Etherington was attempting to shut down the Henry Saloon, a speakeasy located at North Third Street, operated by retired police officer William Howard. When Etherington and the other deputized agents entered the bar to present their warrant, a large crowd gathered around the Henry Saloon. Outnumbered by the crowd, the agents were able to escape through the back door of the saloon. Unfortunately, Etherington got separated from the other agents. He was trapped by Howard, and the surrounding crowd, who began to beat him.

Fearing for his life, Etherington pulled out his gun and shot Howard, wounding him in the abdomen. The crowd grabbed Etherington and continued beating him severely. Newark police arrived, arrested Etherington, and took him to the county jail for his own safety. However, the crowd followed and began to re-form outside the jail. Just one thing was needed to arouse the killing passion, the blood lust, in the mob as it formed early that evening. That was the death of Howard. When the crowd first began to form at the jail, Howard was in the hospital in serious condition. Shortly after 8:00 p.m., the news came that he had died.

With this news came a change in the tone of the mob. Their voices rose to a roar and they began throwing stones at the windows of the jail until not one pane of glass was left unbroken. The guards fired over the heads of the crowd, but they might as well have saved their ammunition. This was a mob that would not listen to pleadings; it wanted action, and action was what it got. Less than two hours after the death of William Howard, the mob broke Etherington out of his second-floor cell and dragged him down the steps of the jail, beating him all the while. Bruised, bleeding, and more terrified than ever, Etherington had a rope placed around his neck. He was pushed

25

The mob used a railroad tie to break down the door of the jail. *Courtesy of the Newark Advocate.*

through the mob for half a block, kicked and beaten every few seconds, while tugging at the rope that was choking him. He begged to be shot, but instead was met with more blows. He was half dead by the time he was brought to the fatal telegraph pole across from the courthouse.

Just before being strung up, Etherington begged for a moment to speak, and he was given permission. He said "Send my love to mother, and tell her that I died in the performance of my duty." Then, without hesitation, he was lynched from the pole. He hung there for about fifteen minutes before the rope broke. Etherington's body fell to the sidewalk, where it was removed and taken to the morgue. It is said that there were several thousand people who witnessed the lynching that evening.

The next day the headline in the *Cleveland Plain Dealer* read *"Ohio Mob Hangs Anti-Saloon League Man."* The paper reported that the mob took the liquor fight into its own hands, hanging an Anti-

Location of hanging pole, marked with X. *Courtesy of the Newark Advocate.*

Saloon League detective from a telegraph pole in the courthouse square after battering down three doors of the jail to get to him.

Eight other Anti-Saloon League detectives, all from Cleveland, had been arrested for assault and battery after the attempted raid and were also locked in the county jail. They escaped probable lynching by being set free by the jailer when renewed threats were heard against them. Fearing that the mob would turn on the jail, the officials released the eight men through a back door, avoiding the possibility of further violence.

A few days after the lynching, 15 people were charged with first-degree murder. Additional indictments were handed down a month later. Four of those indicted were sentenced to serve time in the Ohio Penitentiary. Emolene "Montelle" Watha, and William McKinley were both sentenced to 20 years for manslaughter. They were each released on parole in 1912, after serving just two years. Clarence "Toughy" Timmons served four years of his 15-year sentence. Walter Diehl, the last trial that resulted in a conviction, was given the heaviest sentence of those indicted. He was found guilty of second-degree murder and sentenced to life in prison. However, Governor James Cox pardoned Diehl in 1914, after he had served only three years. No one served more than four years for this terrible crime. Sheriff William Linke and Newark's Mayor Herbert Atherton, were relieved of their duties by Governor Judson Harmon for allowing a lynch mob to take control, and doing little or nothing to stop it. [12]

The following is a list of individuals who were indicted and served time for having a part in the lynching of Carl Etherington:

Ohio Reformatory
John Quency Sutley, 22, glass maker; committed 5/23/1911, paroled 12/31/1912.

Elmer Seary, 19, hostler (stable-boy); committed 5/23/1911, paroled 12/31/1912.

James Richardson, 18, porter; committed 6/26/1911, paroled 2/13/1913.

Edgar Owens, 24, fireman; committed 12/18/11, paroled 3/1/1913.

Robert Cleveland, 26, laborer; committed 3/17/1911, paroled 2/14/1914.

Joe Bush, 23, driver; committed 5/23/1911, paroled 12/31/1912.

Ohio Penitentiary

Emolene "Montelle" Watha, 49, waiter; committed 12/22/1910, paroled 6/19/1913.

Clarence Timmons, 21, laborer; committed 2/20/11 paroled, 11/19/15.

William McKinley, 47, bartender; committed 2/8/1911, paroled 9/1/1913.

Frank Greaf, 43, saloon proprietor; committed 11/16/1911, paroled 11/15/1912.

James Walter Diehl, 26 fireman; committed 10/26/1911, pardoned 1/1/1915.

Suicides in the Jail

Walter Robertson

Walter B. Robertson.
Courtesy of the Newark Advocate.

Suicides are a common occurrence in jails and prisons, and the Licking County jail was no exception. Over the years, several notorious criminals ended their own lives behind these bars.

One such inmate was Walter Robertson, whose story ended tragically on October 23, 1935.

Walter Robertson was born in 1874. In 1895, at the age of 21, he left Licking County and spent a few years out west. To earn his keep, he worked as a farm hand, and at times he would occasionally gamble.

When Walter returned to Licking County in 1900, he was a very wealthy man by the standards of his day. He purchased a 60-acre farm at the intersection of Homer Road and Douglas Lane, between Homer and Centerburg. He invested $2500, and much of his own labor, to build a barn for his livestock and a stall for his horse, Lady. He also remodeled his house, which had previously served as a church and a meeting place.

Although he was well-liked and respected by his friends and neighbors, Walter acquired a reputation as a recluse. While he was out west he learned a few things about magic and dabbled in witchcraft. He got involved with a business partner by the name of Joel Jorgeson. Between the two of them, they had a buried treasure and some personal papers they wanted to keep secret. Walter kept his knowledge of witchcraft secret too, thinking that most people might not understand and would think it strange.

On one occasion, according to Walter, three masked men entered his home one cold rainy night, just as he was getting ready to retire for the evening. They forced him at gunpoint to sign an unknown paper. They said they were in a hurry and that he better sign his name and be quick about it or else he wouldn't live to see another sunrise.

Walter's house near Homer, Ohio.
Courtesy of the Newark Advocate.

No one ever learned the reason for this strange occurrence. It may have involved forcing him to sign over the deed to his property, or reveal the location of the buried treasure that could have contained cash or bank notes.

Soon after settling down on his farm, Walter met a wonderful lady who lived just down the road from him. Jennie Adell Crotinger was her name, but her friends just called her Della. They became good friends and soon he found himself in her company several times a week. After a while, things began to get serious between them.

Many of Walter's neighbors thought he and Della would probably get married someday. It wasn't because Walter didn't try. He asked Della to marry him on several occasions, but she always refused,

Walter Robertson with his horse, Lady.
Courtesy of Russell "Rusty" Robertson.

saying that her father was getting old and needed her to look after him, and that her mother also relied on her to help her out. Of course Walter realized this, but he still wanted to get married. It seemed there was no convincing her, so he decided to let it rest for a while.

Although he usually kept things to himself, Walter did share some secrets with Della, such as his knowledge of witchcraft. He used his knowledge of magic to play tricks on her. One time, he told her that he could stand in his home and make the rocks in her rock garden move using his magic. Late that night he went to her house, rearranged some rocks, and then quietly went back home. He had some people convinced that this wasn't a trick at all, and that he really could make things happen using his magic. Walter knew that if Della ever revealed any of his secrets, it would likely ruin his reputation.

Della's mother, Sara, passed away in 1933, and was buried at the Patterson Cemetery west of Utica on Route 62. Two years later, Walter thought perhaps by this time things might have changed, and this would be a good time to once again ask Della to marry him. He knew she would be at her sister's farm on Friday, October 18, so he decided he would pay her a visit there.

It was no surprise to Della when a crackling sound of broken twigs was followed by Walter's appearance, as making silent or unannounced appearances was one of his talents. As he approached the barn he could see Della milking one of the cows. Walter picked up a milk bucket and began milking another cow. On their way back to the house with the pails of milk, Walter suggested that they step inside the wagon shed to talk, and maybe "pet" for a bit.

Jennie Adell Crotinger.
Courtesy of the Columbus Dispatch.

After a few moments of tender conversation, Walter asked "When will you marry me, dear?" Della responded, "Anytime you say, Walter."

It would seem that this was the answer Walter had for so long hoped to hear. However, with mixed emotion and some degree of anger, he felt a strong sense of resentment. He had asked Della many times in the past and she had always said no. Now he was 61 years old. If they had married when they were young, they could have had a long, happy life together. Perhaps he felt that she was just teasing and not really serious about getting married at all. Or perhaps the answer "yes" when he expected the usual "no" drove him mad.

And what if she let on about all of his secrets that he shared with her? He was not about to take that chance and allow her to humiliate him and destroy his reputation.

Suddenly, something came over him that no one was ever able to fully explain. As he was standing there in a relaxed position, his hand began to grasp a wooden club. Without any warning, Walter picked up the club and hit Della in the head, knocking her to the ground. Della was barely able to move, but still alive and screaming when Walter swung a second blow to the top of her head, fracturing her skull. He turned, dropped the club, and rushed home, leaving Della there to die.

Della's brother-in-law Willard Koontz, who owned the farm, soon found her bleeding and dying on the cold dirt floor of the wagon shed, and called Sheriff Lewis Hague. Sheriff Hague arrived at Walter's home about an hour later and questioned him about Della Crotinger's murder.

Walter seemed to be expecting the officers, as he made no objections while being handcuffed by Deputy Jackson. "Did you kill Jennie Adell Crotinger?" Sheriff Hague asked. Walter responded with "Yes, I killed her, but I don't know why I did." Walter was taken back to the Koontz farm. In the wagon shed where Della's body had just been removed, he responded to questions asked by Deputy McElroy. "Was she sitting or standing?" asked McElroy.
"Standing," Walter said.
"Did she have her back turned, or was she facing you?"
"She was facing me."
"Did you have this planned ahead of time?"
"No, it just happened."
"What time did you arrive here?"
"Around daylight."
"What did you do?"
"I helped Della milk a cow. She milked one and I milked one, and then we came in here." Walter was never able to say exactly why he killed his girlfriend of 35 years.

Walter was arrested and taken to the Licking County jail, where he was placed in a cell on the first floor to await his trial. There were rumors that an angry mob might be planning to break Walter out of jail and lynch him. Walter, fearing for his life, begged the sheriff to move him to another location. Sheriff Hague agreed, not wanting to take any chances and run the risk of another lynching. He made arrangements to have Walter transferred to another unnamed county jail for the weekend for his own safety.

It was later learned he had been taken to Lancaster, Ohio. Soon after being brought back to the Licking County jail to await his trial, Walter began to show evidence of a mental collapse. Later his condition was described by three physicians— Dr. Baxter, Dr. Lewis Mitchell, and Dr. Homer J. Davis, all appointed by the Licking County Probate Court— as a sham. They all agreed that Walter was sane, and responsible for his deed.

Sheriff Hague holds the murder weapon.
Courtesy of the Columbus Dispatch.

On October 23, 1935, at the age of 61, Walter Robertson hanged himself in his first-floor cell. He made a rope from strips of his blanket, made a noose on one end, and tied the other end to an upper cell bar. His body was found slumped in a grotesque, distorted position within his cell the following morning by James Pursley, a fellow prisoner, and Deputy Sheriff John Widrig.

Miss Crotinger was buried next to her mother at the Patterson Cemetery. Her father James, who died in 1936, a year after Della's murder, is buried there as well. Walter Robertson was buried in the Centerburg Cemetery.

Walter had two brothers. Delos (or Lue, as he was called), lived in California. He died mysteriously, with his body found head first in a rain barrel. No one knew for sure if this was suicide, an accident, or murder. Frank Robertson was Walter's other brother. He lived just a few miles north of Walter. Walter's sister, Grace Keller, lived near Mt. Vernon, Ohio. She became the administrator of Walter's estate. [13]

George Hackett

Other notable suicides in the jail include George Hackett, who hanged himself in the jail in 1904.

Hackett was being held in the county jail while awaiting trial for shooting his wife at their home. He claimed that he only intended to wound her. Hackett was bound over by the grand jury, and since that time had become very despondent, sitting for hours in a chair with his head buried in his hands. He seemed to have a mortal fear of standing trial for the crime he had committed. He was known to be a suicide risk and had already attempted to kill himself once— a couple of weeks earlier, he put disinfectant used in rat poison in a cup of water and drank it, but the solution was diluted too much and only made him sick.

On Wednesday morning, April 27, Hackett was found hanging from the bars of his cell. Apparently he had been dead only a short time when he was found, as his body was still warm. He had used a broken bottle to cut a piece of rope about four feet long out of the side of his cot and attached one end to an upper bar in his cell. He made a noose on the other end, and then strangled himself by slowly sinking to his knees.

Hackett was just 37 years old. He left a note addressed to whoever found his body, filled with messages of loving farewell to his wife, and orders about the disposal of his body. The note was written in a clear and legible handwriting as follows:

"To who finds my body:

I am not guilty of shooting my wife with intent to kill. When I did that deed I did not know what I was doing, I had taken a poison and it made me crazy, and that is I how I came to do that deed. Please send these words to her. Darling I loved you sweet. I never did do, but you believed others, but I leave them in the hands of God. I have been accused of things I never did do. Dear wife, I have loved you and have always loved you. I have told you that nothing but death could separate us, and it has done it. Remember dear wife, remember me darling wife. Good bye, dear Helen. Good bye sweet

Helen. P.S. Send my body to J.M. Jones, Granville, OH, my wife has my life insurance papers."

Coroner C. F. Loggo was notified of Hackett's death and went immediately to the jail to take charge of the body and personal effects. Among his personal items were a number of letters asking those to whom they were addressed to go to his wife and ask her not to appear against him. [14]

Martin Kelley

In June of 1905, Martin Kelley was found wandering around nude in Newton Township, just north of Newark. He was brought to Newark and placed in the county jail to await a hearing by the probate judge on a charge of lunacy.

After spending just two days in jail, Martin Kelley committed suicide in the bathing area on the second floor. He cut his throat with a razor that he obtained from Samuel Bucklew, a fellow inmate. After getting the razor, he stepped into the bathing area and slit his throat. The suicide occurred around 9:30 Monday morning, while the jailer was in his office below. Several prisoners called to the jailer, stating that Kelley had cut his throat and was bleeding to death. The officer ran to the bathing area where he observed a horrible sight. On the tile floor of the room, writhing in his death struggles, blood spurting from an ugly gash in his neck, the prisoner was gasping for breath. It was obvious that he had only a few moments to live. With the help of one of the prisoners, the officer moved him from the bathing area to the corridor and called Dr. C. F. Legge. After the arrival of the physician, Kelley lived only a few moments. The coroner's results indicated that he committed suicide while suffering from dementia. [15]

Four days later, the *Newark Advocate* reported that this was a case of mistaken identity, and Martin Kelley was alive and well. Patrick Kelley, Martin's brother, was called to Newark to identify the dead man. He stated that while the body resembled his brother in some respects, there were certain peculiar marks lacking which convinced him that it was not his brother. Further proof that Martin Kelley was still alive and well came from his wife in Adelaide,

Pennsylvania, who telephoned a sister and said that her husband was there and had not been in Newark for weeks.

It was then believed that a man by the name of Jake Boyer might have murdered an old woman named Frances Werts. When Boyer was picked up for wandering around nude, he gave the authorities a false name of Martin Kelley. This story began to unravel after Martin Kelley's landlady, Mrs. Stella Porter, called the police chief's office and stated that the name of the dead man was familiar, and that a man by that name boarded with her aunt at Martin's Ferry. In the company of a police officer, Mrs. Porter and her aunt visited the funeral home where the body was awaiting burial. They recognized the features of the dead man as being those of the former Martin's Ferry resident.

It was eventually determined that Martin Kelley was, in fact, the man who had committed suicide in the bathing area of the jail. Apparently, Patrick Kelley had denied that this was his brother so as to not disgrace the family name. Bucklew, who had provided Kelley with the razor, later died from intoxication on September 24, 1907, while still in the jail. He was 53 years old. [16]

Earl Johnson

On June 3, 1916 Earl Johnson, age 19, died of a previously self-inflicted gunshot wound to his head while being held in a first-floor jail cell. Johnson, a laborer, had gone to the Woods Avenue home where his wife was employed, with intentions of killing her. He was refused entry and a call was made for police to arrive. When the police approached Johnson, he started to run and then hesitated in the alley long enough to fire a bullet into his head. Police Chief Sheridan was not more than 40 feet away when the shot was fired. Although he called to Johnson not to shoot, his warning did no good. Johnson was taken to the Newark Sanitarium with a .32 caliber bullet in his head. His wound did not appear to be very serious, and officials at the Sanitarium said he had "a fair chance of recovery." After being treated for his wounds, he was taken to the county jail.

He was held there at his own request because he said he feared for his life, thinking that a rum runner gang was after him.

Although he was expected to recover, Earl Johnson later died at the jail from his self-inflicted injury and was buried at Cedar Hill Cemetery. From a note left by Johnson before shooting himself, it was evident that he was suffering from a distorted mind. In the note, which was addressed to the public, he blamed domestic trouble for his actions and expressed a wish to be buried alongside his wife, whom he had intended to kill. He also claimed to have $365 buried or hidden somewhere but would not disclose its location. Several weeks earlier, Johnson had called upon his newly married sister-in-law. He said he had a wedding present for her and when told to bring it in, he hurled a stone through the window of her house. For this, he was fined and ordered to pay for the broken window. [17]

Walter Loyd Priest

On August 11, 1930, Walter Loyd Priest, 47, committed suicide while his cellmates were asleep by hanging himself from a beam in his cell using a strand of rope. He was discovered by Deputy L. D. Hague when he opened the cell block on the third floor. Another prisoner in the cell told Sheriff Festus Hoover that Priest had been given a drink of water around midnight and that he was all right at that time.

Walter Priest was the son of Mr. and Mrs. George W. Priest of Reform, Ohio. He worked as a lineman for the Postal Telegraph Company until he entered the army and served in World War I. [18] He had been brought to the Licking County jail from Mount Vernon by Deputy C. W. Pletcher. He had asked the sheriff there for protection from a gang of rum runners who he stated were after him. Sheriff Hoy C. Lynde of Knox County notified the local county officials that Priest, while talking to him about getting protection, suddenly ducked into a corner when a passing vehicle drove by. He told the sheriff that he ducked to avoid the gunfire from the vehicle. Priest was brought to the Licking County jail for safekeeping, a measure sometimes taken to protect someone from harm from themselves, or others. John O. Thompson, the county coroner, viewed the body and officially pronounced death due to hanging. It was believed that Priest may have been suffering from shellshock as a result of his World War I service, and this might have caused him to take his life.

Mae Varner

On Tuesday, July 14, 1953, 55-year-old Mae Varner attempted to commit suicide at her home at 28 East Harrison Street in Newark by taking an overdose of sleeping pills. She was rushed to the Newark Hospital where doctors were able to revive her by pumping her stomach. She was then taken to the county jail for safekeeping. She was taken to the fourth-floor cell block for women, where she would remain until she could get the help she needed.

Apparently, Mrs. Varner had a book of matches with her and used it to set her clothes on fire. By the time she was discovered by Matron Marie Thompson, her clothes were virtually burned off of her body as she was lying on the cot in her cell. She was discovered just 45 minutes after being brought to the jail while the Matron was making her hourly check of the fourth-floor cells. Mrs. Varner was rushed to the hospital once again, where she died that morning. In spite of her taking her own life, her death was ruled accidental by Dr. M. H. Koehler, the county coroner. [19]

Albert McClain

Another incident occurred in 1961 with inmate Albert McClain. McClain, 43, was the son of Charles and Atlanta Kerns McClain. He was an employee of the Burke Golf Club Company and a former mental patient at the Columbus State Hospital. [20] He had been brought to the jail on a charge of intoxication and was being held for safekeeping. Three days before he was to be returned to the Columbus State Hospital for a final hearing on his release, he took his belt, tied one end to the top bunk of a double-tiered bed, placed a noose around his neck, and hanged himself. He was found hanging dead in his third-floor jail cell by Deputy Sheriff Jack Jones early on the morning of Friday, September 22. The death was ruled a self-inflicted hanging by Licking County Coroner K. P. Scott. McClain's death came one week after a nomination by the Licking County Grand Jury that mental patients should not be confined in ordinary jail cells.

Commission president Herbert Koontz said that the problem of housing mental patients would be discussed at the commissioners' meeting. Sheriff William McElroy told newsmen that he had long been opposed to housing mental patients in the county jail, but had no other choice. Captain Richard Fitzsimmons, Chief of Deputy Sheriffs, said that it was general practice to take belts and shoelaces away from those charged with intoxication or being held for safekeeping, but that this was not done in McClain's case, and the matter would be investigated.

Attempted Suicide

Besides these suicides, there was an unsuccessful attempt at suicide on March 10, 1962. Robert Kopp, who was arrested for trying to cash a forged check in a downtown Newark bank, attempted to hang himself. The cries for help from a prisoner arrested earlier on an intoxication charge alerted Sergeant George Campbell and Patrolman Carl Rinehart in the radio room. They found Kopp hanging from an electric wire attached to a support beam in his jail cell at 6:00 p.m. Rinehart cut the unconscious prisoner down and administered artificial respiration. Kopp was completely revived and rushed to the hospital where he was examined and released to police custody. In the police report it was stated that Kopp had apparently pulled the electrical cord from the ceiling of the jail. He tied one end to a beam, and then made a noose around his neck with the other end of the cord. [21]

Jail Damage

In December 1975, Karen Fry, who had a lot of extra time on her hands while serving time for child neglect, devised a plan to get out of her fourth-floor cell. This was not a plan to escape, but instead to join three male inmates in the cell below. It must have been a difficult task, but with a lot of determination, hard work, and the help of the three inmates below, Fry was able to chip a hole through eight inches of concrete, using only a broom handle and coat hangers.

However, while the hole in the ceiling of the third-floor cell was 36 inches in diameter, the hole on the fourth floor was just 8 inches in diameter, and not yet large enough for Fry to slip through. The opening went unnoticed for some time, but was finally discovered by deputies on December 9. The four inmates— Daniel Soloway, Arthur Holman, Rufus Fields, and Karen Fry— were charged with criminal damage to the Licking County jail. Today you can still see two steel beams in the ceiling of cell #1 on the third floor, where repairs were made to reinforce the area where the large hole once was.

Pleas given on jail damage

The four prisoners entered pleas in municipal court on charges of criminal damage to the Licking County Jail. Daniel Soloway, 21, of Newport, Kentucky and Arthur Holmann, 25, of Newark, Ohio pled innocent. John Taylor, the municipal court judge, returned them to jail in lieu of $10,000 bonds. Rufus Fields, of Columbus, Ohio, pled guilty. Judge Taylor sentenced him to 90 days in jail, fined him $500, and suspended all but 10 days and $250. Karen Fry pled no contest, and was found guilty by Judge Taylor. He delayed sentencing until 3:00 p.m., January 21. Taylor allowed her to sign a

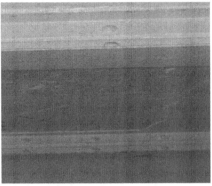

Beams installed in ceiling of third floor cell to repair damage from hole caused by inmates.

recognizance bond for her release on this charge, although she was not scheduled to be released from jail until February 1 on her child neglect conviction. [22]

Jail Cell Fire Set by Inmate

On Friday, May 30, 1975, a fire broke out in one of the cells at the Licking County jail, causing minor damage to one of the mattresses. Sheriff's deputies said the fire was set at 6:30 p.m. by a prisoner who put a match to the mattress. Cruisers on patrol throughout the county were immediately ordered to return to the jail in case prisoners had to be evacuated. However, the fire was extinguished before Newark firemen arrived. [23]

A similar incident occurred three years later. On Monday, June 12, 1978, Licking County sheriff's deputies evacuated the second floor of the jail when a prisoner set fire to a mattress in one of the cells. Eight prisoners were evacuated and forced to stand in the north yard of the jail with their hands above their heads against the building.

Deputies and Newark police armed with shotguns guarded the prisoners while firefighters doused the burning mattress. Although the fire was extinguished in just a few minutes, there were 12 firefighters and 6 pieces of firefighting equipment on hand. As the prisoners stood outside in the rain that day, under heavy guard, some shouted and joked and discussed escape plans. But with their arms and legs spread out against the black stone wall, no one made an attempt to escape. [24]

Murderers of Licking County

The Death of Frances Werts

"McKean Township Woman Victim of Shocking Tragedy Early Thursday Morning." That was the headline in the *Newark Advocate* on June 2, 1905, the day after Mrs. Frances Werts was mysteriously and brutally murdered in her home, her head and face horribly crushed by a large club. Mrs. Werts lived about seven miles northwest of Newark, on a small farm in McKean township with her granddaughter, Eva Werts. It was this 14-year girl who was able to escape and run a quarter of a mile across fields of corn and oats to John Schimp, a neighbor, where she told about her grandmother's murder. Schimp fetched another neighbor, and the three returned to the Werts' home. Upon arriving at the scene of the murder, a horrible sight presented itself. At the foot of the stairway lay the dead body of Mrs. Werts. By her side was a three-tine pitchfork, with which she had attempted to defend herself. Her body was covered from head to foot with blood. The pitchfork was also covered with blood, from the tip of the handle to the end of the tines. The woman's head was one solid mass of crushed bones, bruised flesh, and blood clotted with her hair.

At the head of the stairs, the coroner found the murder weapon, a club four feet in length, covered with blood and hair. Further investigation revealed that the room had been hurriedly searched. The bureau drawer was found open and several articles were missing including a revolver, and several valuable papers.

Eva Werts was the only eyewitness to the crime. She saw the murderer strike the first blow, and heard repeated blows while making her escape from the house. Eva heard her grandmother's last cries for help while she was hurrying from the yard to Mr. Schimp's house. As she relayed her story to a reporter for the *Newark Advocate,* Eva said:

"Grandma and I were awakened last night about 1 o'clock by unusual noises around the house...We could hear someone in the kitchen and Grandma remarked that it was strange that the dog didn't bark. We always kept the dog there, and he is counted one of the crossest dogs in the neighborhood, and I told Grandma that if anyone was in the room, he would be barking. We reached the foot of the stairs and tried to force the door open, but it was held by someone on the other side of the door in the kitchen. Both of us pushed against the door, but could not open it. Grandma told me to go upstairs and call to the neighbors for help...When I got no answer, I returned to the stairway, the door at the bottom was open and I could see the arm and shoulder of a man, but not his face.

...I could see the big club in his hand. Just as I reached the top of the stairs, after calling for help, I saw him strike at grandma with a stick. I heard the blow fall and Grandma said: "Eva, I'm gone now." I ran to the front window and crawled out on the top of the little front porch. All this time I could hear the man pounding Grandmother with the club. I jumped down from the roof of the porch and ran to the side yard and around the orchard, westward to the home of John Schimp. There I told him about the man killing Grandma, and he dressed and we went to Mr. Nash's home. His wife was afraid to stay at home alone and he couldn't go with us. We then went to Mr. Foster's home and got him. We three then returned to Grandma's home."

During the testimony, Eva was asked if she knew who the murderer was. She stated that she did not know for sure who murdered her grandmother, but thought it might be Levi Bevard, a close neighbor of the Werts family. Officers said that, aside from the accusation made by Eva Werts, they had much circumstantial evidence against Bevard. It was noted that footprints followed by bloodhounds were the same size as Bevard's boots. Frances Werts had a 109-acre farm; Bevard's wife was one of two heirs. When a financial transaction involving $100 was discovered between Bevard and Mrs. Werts, it raised even more suspicion. Although no one was ever found guilty of the murder, Levi Bevard was a strong suspect and was even held in the Licking County jail for a period of time. [25]

Child Rapist and Murderer Donald Moreland

On March 31, 1911, Samuel Fravel, a local merchant, was driving out to his farm when he discovered a body by the side of the road. The body was that of 14-year-old Elsie Henthorn, who lived about three miles north of Pataskala in Licking County. She had been shot through the breast and dumped by the roadside.

Elsie had last been seen getting a ride home from school with a man named Donald Moreland, who was believed to have mental health issues and possibly be demented. Moreland was found a couple of hours later hiding in a barn on the farm of John Fravel, Samuel's brother. He was arrested and taken to the Licking County jail by Sheriff Frank Slabaugh.

Moreland told arresting officer Marshal Howard Cooper that Elsie's death was an accident. "I thought pretty well of the girl and we quarreled. She had my revolver in her lap, and during the struggle to get possession of the gun it went off and she died." After further questioning, however, Moreland admitted that he was drunk and had attempted to rape Elsie after getting her in the buggy. He then confessed to shooting her while she was fighting off his attacks. The prosecutor accepted a plea bargain of manslaughter and Moreland was sent to the Ohio State Reformatory in Mansfield. [26]

Safe Robbers Gun Down Officer in Cold Blood

Newark city patrolman Harry Beasley was walking his downtown beat on Tuesday evening June 30, 1931, when he was gunned down by an armed gang attempting to steal the safe from a local shoe store.

It was shortly after 9:00 p.m. and Officer Beasley had just begun his shift, which would have lasted until 1:00 a.m. He turned off of

Patrolman Harry C. Beasley. *Courtesy of the Newark Police Department.*

South Third Street toward the alley that ran east and west behind the South Park Place stores. As Beasley approached the corner, he saw a car facing west in the alley with the engine running and the headlights on. A gang of men had used a small wrecking bar to force open the rear door of the Newark Bargain Shoe Store. They had taken $5.05 from the cash register and were attempting to steal the safe, which contained another $500, when Beasley interrupted them.

With the headlights glaring in his eyes, Beasley was unable to identify the men. Without any warning the men began to shoot at him, firing their weapons in rapid succession. Beasley was struck twice as he fell to the ground. One bullet entered the right side of his chest, passing through his lung and lodging near his spine. The other hit his right foot, shattering the bones.

In spite of his injuries, Beasley had the presence of mind to pull his Colt .45 revolver from its holster and empty all six rounds into the darkness in the direction of the gunfire. It is not known if Beasley hit either of the gunmen. The bullets from Beasley's gun took an upward course and two of them lodged in the rear of the Newark Bargain Shoe Store and the Cornell Store. The robbers dropped the safe, ran to their car, and sped westward out of the alley, south to the market alley, and west to Third Street where they disappeared.

Beasley was able to talk after being taken to the hospital and told police that all he could see in the dark alley was the flash of gunfire after he stepped into the car's headlights. He was not able to

48

Fellow officers carry Beasley's coffin.
Courtesy of the Licking County Historical Society.

provide information about the identity of the robbers or the make of the automobile, leaving the police without a clue to work from. Two days later, on July 2, 1931, Harry Beasley died from his wounds. His murder was never solved and to this day the identity of his killers remains unknown.

Born on November 1, 1889, Beasley enlisted in the Navy in 1910, and served on several ships of the Atlantic Fleet. He participated in the Battle of Veracruz in April, 1914 while serving on the USS Florida, and was awarded the Medal of Honor for gallantry in action. He left the Navy soon after this battle but re-enlisted at the outbreak of World War I, and served until 1921.

In 1926, Beasley began a second career with the Newark Police Department. He served as a member of the police department for five years, during which time he was decorated with medals for marksmanship. He was a member of the Veterans of Foreign Wars, and the Fraternal Order of Police.

Harry Beasley's flag-draped coffin.
Courtesy of the Licking County Historical Society.

Following his death, his Medal of Honor was donated by surviving relatives and is on permanent display at the Newark police station. Harry Beasley will always be remembered as a true hero, one of Newark's finest police officers. [27]

Pataskala Farmer Shot to Death

Pataskala farmer Finley Fry was shot to death late one evening when an intruder was able to gain access to his home through a side window. The intruder went upstairs, where Fry and his wife were in bed. Just as the intruder shined his light on Fry, Mrs. Fry turned a lamp on and called to the man "What are you doing here?" He mumbled a reply and then a shot rang out, striking Mr. Fry in the arm. Almost immediately a second shot was fired, this time striking Fry in the head. After firing the second shot, the man ran out of the house and escaped in a car he and his brother had stolen.

Later, when Sheriff Lewis Hague and Deputy Sheriff William McElroy arrived, Mrs. Fry told them that the intruder said "You stole our farm," just before he fired the first shot. The farm referred to was purchased from a bank in an estate settlement 10 years earlier.

While Licking County deputy sheriffs were aided by state police, other law enforcement officers searched the countryside in half a dozen central Ohio counties. A few hours later, word came from Cumberland, Maryland— about 240 miles east of Newark— of the arrest of 17-year-old Walter E. Hendricks and his brother, 19-year-old Alvertus Hendricks. The Cumberland police located the stolen car they were driving broken down along the roadside, with the rifle used in the murder in the back seat.

The men were taken into custody and questioned by Cumberland police. After being questioned about the rifle, the two admitted to stealing the car and shooting Finley Fry. They were brought back to Newark and taken to the Licking County jail by Sheriff Hague and Deputy Sheriff McElroy. Alvertus and Walter Hendricks were charged with murder on October 16, 1938, by authority of the sheriff. Alvertus was discharged on January 31, 1939, by authority of the U.S. Marshall. Walter was discharged on December 9, 1938, by order of the prosecutor, and sent to the Lima Correctional Prison for the Criminally Insane. [28]

The Four Mile Lock Inn Murderer

On the evening of November 3, 1938, a call from an unidentified individual was received at the Criss Brothers Funeral Home. The caller told Richard Criss to send an ambulance to the Four Mile Lock Inn, located between Hebron and Heath. Sheriff Hague was also notified of a shooting at the inn.

When the sheriff and the deputies arrived, they found 46-year-old Mrs. Mattie Nies on the ground suffering from gunshot wounds to the head and chest. A second shooting victim, Donald Hatfield, was discovered just a few feet away. Blood covered the floor, a table, and the bar. Two blood trails led through the inn, one to the cash register, the other out the front door. As the two victims were rushed to the hospital, the sheriff and his deputies began a manhunt. With their guns drawn and lanterns lighting the way, the sheriff and his deputies began sweeping the fields and woods in the area. Just a few minutes later, they encountered a man in the field by a creek. He was identified as Mark Heck, age 50. When Deputy McElroy searched Heck, he found three empty .22 caliber shells in his pocket. Heck had thrown the gun into the muddy creek, but forgot he had placed the shells in his pocket.

After Heck was taken to jail the deputies were able to locate a witness by the name of R. F. Dufford. As Sheriff Hague interviewed Heck, the story became clear. Mrs. Nies operated the Four Mile Lock Inn. She had employed Mark Heck for a while, but dismissed him. Six months later, while working at a gas station near Mt. Vernon, the anger of his firing began to get the better of him. With revenge on his mind, he went to the inn where he was greeted by Mrs. Nies and Donald Hatfield, a customer. They invited Heck to stay for something to eat and drink. While dining at a table, Mrs. Nies got up and walked to the cash register. Heck jumped up, pulled his gun, and fired two shots, striking Mrs. Nies in the head and chest. As Hatfield got up to offer assistance, Heck shot him in his side, not wanting any witnesses.

Heck ran to the woods, but then returned to the scene of the crime to make sure he had accomplished what he went there for. R. F. Dufford pulled up in his car to offer assistance, but Heck pulled his gun and told Dufford "Unless you want some of the same, you'd better just drive on." Dufford sped away but stopped down the road and called the sheriff. Heck, knowing now that there was a witness, fled into the fields and woods. By early morning the sheriff and deputies had all they needed to charge Heck with attempted murder. The sheriff went to the hospital hoping to be able to talk to the victims, but Hatfield had died of his injuries overnight. Instead of filing an affidavit for attempted murder, Heck would now be charged with murder. Less than one month later, Mrs. Nies died. Now Mark Heck would be facing a charge for double murder.

Paul House, who was appointed by the court to serve as Heck's attorney, was given five days to draw up a formal plea concerning Heck's sanity at the time of the murder. House said Heck requested a trial by jury, and Judge Slabaugh indicated a jury list would be drawn after the insanity plea was investigated. In the meantime, Heck was being held in the Licking County jail.

At the trial, Mark Heck was found guilty and almost sent to the electric chair. Instead, he was sentenced to life in the Columbus Ohio Penitentiary. Judge Slabaugh ordered that every year on November 3, the anniversary of the crime, Heck was to be placed in solitary confinement to reflect on what he had done. Some might say that this was a better form of punishment than the death penalty, since his punishment would last for the rest of his life. [29]

The Handsaw Slayer

Licking County has had its share of murders over the years, but the one on January 6, 1947, was the most gruesome ever recorded in county history. This is the tale of Laura Belle Devlin, also known as the "Handsaw Slayer."

Thomas Devlin came to this country from Ireland in 1899. He was employed with the United States Steel Company in Ambridge, Pennsylvania. He married Laura Belle in Pittsburgh on April 7, 1907. After moving to Newark, Ohio, they bought a house located at 78 King Avenue, across from where Newark High School is today.

For many years their marriage was a happy one, but it seems the years took their

Thomas Devlin. *Courtesy of the Licking County Records and Archives Department.*

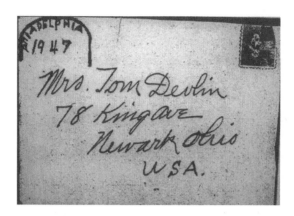

toll and arguments became more common. By 1947, 40 years had slipped away since they first fell in love and got married. Thomas and Laura were now both 72 years old. They argued frequently and over time these arguments began to turn violent. One evening, during dinner, an argument escalated and got out of control. Mr. Devlin became so upset with his wife that he picked up his dinner plate and threw it at her. Tensions were already high, and for Laura this was the last straw. She attacked Thomas with a small knife, but that didn't seem to do any good, so she began pounding him with her fists, eventually knocking him out cold. While Thomas was lying unconscious on the floor, Mrs. Devlin went to the garage where she found a sickle and a handsaw. Wearing a stocking cap and an old coat, she began hacking her husband's body with the sickle until it broke. She then picked up the handsaw and began dissecting her husband, cutting off his arms, legs and head.

So, what do you do with a body after it has been cut up into pieces? Well, Laura tossed the torso in a field next to her home and set it on fire. She then put some of the body parts, including Thomas's head, in her wood stove, and cooked other parts in her kitchen stove.

Laura had a plan that would explain the disappearance of her husband. She wrote a letter meant to look like it came from Thomas's cousin in Philadelphia, where he was supposedly visiting. The letter stated that both the cousin's mother and Thomas had died and were being taken to Ireland to be buried with other family members.

The postman became suspicious that something wasn't right when he hadn't seen Mr. Devlin for several days. When he confronted Laura about where her husband was, she showed him the letter. The postman noticed that the stamp had been hand-printed and the letter had not gone through the mail. He suggested that she show the envelope to the police.

When the police became involved they also noticed that the postmark was hand-printed and the stamp appeared to be drawn on the envelope. They became suspicious of the contents of the letter, and went to the Devlin house. Within a few minutes of their arrival, detectives discovered small piles of human ashes in the back yard. Further investigation revealed an unburned portion of Mr. Devlin's torso in a field next to the home. They also found fragments of skull, and a large rug covered with blood where Laura had apparently placed Thomas's body as she hacked it to pieces. Confronted by this evidence, Mrs. Devlin, who had been taken to police headquarters, calmly admitted beating her husband about the head with her fists, then disposing of his body. She said "Thomas had threatened to kill me so many times that I just decided to end it all, so I attacked him with a small knife, but that didn't work so I pounded him with my fists." When she finished her story, she asked "May I go home now?" While being processed in at the county jail, Mrs. Devlin put up a fuss while being fingerprinted, saying "Don't do that it will make my hands dirty." She also complained about having her picture taken. After being arrested and booked, she was charged with homicide due to senile dementia. She was later transported to the Lima State Prison for the Criminally Insane for psychiatric evaluation. She died there of pneumonia just three weeks later, on January 29, 1947.

For obvious reasons the Devlin house was later torn down. Only an innocent looking empty grass lot is visible there today, a hundred yards or so west of Newark High School. [30]

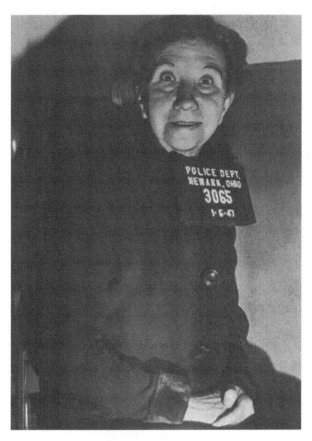

Laura Devlin's mugshot.
Courtesy of thepostmortempost.com

The Love Slaying

Frank Rizzo (left) and Joanne Thomas (right). *Courtesy of the Newark Advocate.*

Joanne Thomas was a pretty, 25-year-old brunette who lived with her mother and stepfather, Mr. and Mrs. Griggs Brehm, on Hudson Avenue in Newark, Ohio. She graduated from Newark High School in 1944. Joanne was a factory worker at Owens Corning Fiberglas Corporation, and had been a waitress in several Newark restaurants, as well as in Columbus.

Her boyfriend, Frank Rizzo, was a handsome, 30-year-old man who had graduated from Newark High School in 1940. He attended Kent State University, and was a veteran of World War II. Frank worked for his brother Tony, who owned the Producers Market at 39 South Fifth Street in Newark, and had been dating Joanne for five years.

It was a warm and beautiful Saturday afternoon on September 15, 1951. Joanne Thomas had purchased a .22 caliber target pistol the Thursday before from a local hardware store. Saturday morning, she came back downtown at about 11:00 a.m. with the intention of returning the gun to the store. However, when she arrived at the store, she changed her mind and decided to keep the gun after all. Joanne then went to a downtown tavern and had a couple of drinks. When she left the tavern, she called a taxi and had the driver take her to the Waterworks Road area. This was an area north of town, with few houses around at that time. As she got out of the taxi, she told the driver to come back and pick her up in about 15 minutes. Apparently, she was planning on doing some target practice, but the only shot that was fired was when the gun went off accidentally while she was loading it.

The Producers Market. *Courtesy of the Newark Advocate.*

When the cab driver returned, she had him take her to North Fifth and West Main Street. From there she walked to the Producers Market. She removed the gun from her purse as she entered the store and walked over to the fruit stand where Frank Rizzo was working. Frank was weighing grapes for a customer and had his back turned when Joanne called his name. As Frank turned around, she fired four shots in rapid succession into his chest and stomach. As the bullets pierced his body, one narrowly missed his heart. As he slumped over helplessly onto the floor, Joanne turned to his brother, handed the gun to him, and said "Tony, now you shoot me." Joanne then ran to Frank's side, knelt down beside him, and cried brokenly, "I love you, I love you, Frank." This dramatic fatal shooting took place at 1:30 p.m. in front of a half-dozen startled witnesses.

Joanne Thomas was taken into custody by police as she was bending over her boyfriend's body, repeatedly professing her love for him. She was questioned by police Chief Arthur Jones, Assistant Prosecutor Roderic Jones, and Sheriff William McElroy. She admitted to the shooting, claiming that Rizzo had been cheating on her. She said the two of them had been dating for five years, but lately she had noticed a coolness in his affection for her.

Joanne told police that she and Frank had had a date Wednesday night, but he didn't show up. She said that she was walking by a local tavern that night, and saw Frank seated with another girl. Apparently, Joanne became upset and irrational when she found out Frank was dating another woman. She told Chief Jones that she had never before fired any kind of weapon. Chief Jones said that several times during her talk with police Joanne broke down, saying that she loved Frank. Joanne was later found not guilty by reason of insanity. She was sent to the Lima Ohio State Hospital for the Criminally Insane. Records show that she was released just one year later. [31]

The Route 40 Hitchhike Slayers

What is it that makes someone want to kill another person? There are some circumstances, such as self-defense, that might justify such actions, but what makes someone kill an innocent person who was just trying to help?

It is impossible to say what gets into someone's head that makes them harm an innocent person, but that is what happened to a taxi driver who only wanted to help a couple of young servicemen.

On March 4, 1952, two 18-year-old Marines, Louis Allen Angel of Huntington, West Virginia, and Harmon Cordray of Mooresville, Indiana, went AWOL from a naval hospital in South Carolina. They made their way to Ohio and that Tuesday morning they were hitchhiking along Route 40, just east of Kirkersville, when Allen Drake, a taxi driver, passed them by. He drove down the road about 400 yards, turned around, went back, and offered the two men a ride to Columbus. As they approached Kirkersville, the men told him to stop. They then beat him with a blackjack nightstick, stunning him. As Drake began to revive, Louis Angel fired a shot in front of him from the passenger seat, just to scare him. The bullet went through

Louis Allen Angel and Harmon Cordray.
Courtesy of the Newark Advocate.

the front window of the cab, while Drake ducked, rolled out of the cab, and ran to the left rear of the car. Angel jumped out of the car and approached Drake, who was crouched up near the rear wheel. Angel pointed his revolver at Drake and pulled the trigger. The two men then drove away in the car, leaving Drake there to die. They later abandoned the car near Drake's home.

The identity of the two men was learned after a concerted effort from various law enforcement agencies. It was learned that they had stayed at the Arcade Hotel visiting girls from St. Louisville with whom they were acquainted. The two were arrested in the vicinity of their hometowns on Friday, March 7, 1952. The witness identifying them was a Columbus man who found Drake dying along Route 40.

On Saturday, March 8, 1952, Angel and Cordray confessed to killing Drake and were charged with first-degree murder. Charges were filed by Licking County Sheriff William McElroy and Highway Patrolman John Wessler in the Court of Keith Lowery of Hebron, Ohio. The two men were incarcerated at the Licking County jail.

On Sunday, March 9, 1952, the trigger-man, Louis Angel, made an unsuccessful attempt at suicide while in solitary confinement. He used a broken light bulb to try and cut an artery in his left arm just above a cast he was wearing, due to a broken hand from a fist fight several weeks earlier. He was found lying in a pool of blood after other inmates heard him moaning, and was taken to the Newark Hospital under guard, repeatedly telling officers that he would not stand trial. He was treated at the hospital and returned to jail, where he was closely guarded as a suicide risk.

Although Angel and Cordray had confessed, they later pled not guilty. They were granted separate trials for what became known as the "Highway Murder." Louis Angel was convicted and sentenced to die in the electric chair. After the verdict, he was reported to have been in a jovial mood. Harmon Cordray, who testified that Angel was the shooter, was found not guilty and acquitted on June 7, 1952. He was sent back to the Marines and was placed in solitary confinement for being involved in this incident. He was later sent to fight in the Korean War, and died on September 4, 1976.

Angel was able to get two different stays of execution. However, on Friday, January 24, 1953, Louis Allen Angel was executed in the electric chair at the Ohio Penitentiary in Columbus. This was the first crime in Licking County where the death penalty was imposed and carried out. [32]

Harold Shackelford: Crazed by Liquor

It was said that Harold Shackelford was a man who was crazed by liquor. Indicted for first-degree murder in the strangulation and beating death of 51-year-old Miss Mary Dunn, of 42 North Buena Vista Street, Shackelford was transferred from the city jail to the county jail to await his arraignment.

The brutal murder of Miss Dunn took place at 5:45 a.m. on Sunday, September 16, 1956, when Shackleford attacked her as she was on her way to Blessed Sacrament Church. Reports indicate that he strangled her, along with breaking most of her ribs. Although he denied that he attempted to rape her, police found her clothing had been almost completely removed. She had also been beaten beyond recognition.

The primary clue that helped police establish Shackelford as the man they were looking for was a pair of heavy-rimmed eyeglasses found at 248 East Main Street, where the murder took place. Shackelford admitted to detectives that he had lost a pair of glasses that evening.

When first picked up, Shackelford gave an account of his whereabouts up until an hour before the killing. He had been at a party with other people who brought him home around 5:00 a.m. "I should have stayed home" he said, as he confessed to police and Prosecutor Forrest Ashcraft. He said he intended to go to the State Restaurant when he saw Miss Dunn coming across the railroad tracks. He said "I had no reason for hitting her, and I don't know why I did, no reason… no reason." He did admit to having a lot to drink at the party, and said that "when I get drunk, I just get mean." Apparently, it was true that Shackelford was "crazed by liquor."

This was not the first time Shackelford had committed a serious crime. He had just been paroled from San Quentin prison in California, where he served five years and nine months of his ten-year sentence for the near fatal beating of a woman in San Francisco. After assaulting this woman, he had left her for dead. Other convictions included purse snatching, for which he served one year in a California county jail. Originally a native of Newark, he also had a juvenile record in Ohio.

He paid the ultimate price for his crimes on June 24, 1957 when he was put to death by the electric chair at the Ohio Penitentiary in Columbus. [33]

A Family Destroyed

Author's Note: the following account was written by Kevin Bennett. It was published in the Newark Advocate *on January 9, 2014, and is printed here with permission.*

Herman and Carol Jean Leasure operated a 190-acre farm north of Granville on Burg Street. They had two sons, 17-year-old David and 15-year-old Danny Joe. The boys were well liked by their peers and teachers, and Danny was considered quiet and shy. Beneath this calm facade, however, were tensions that eventually caused him to gun down both of his parents on the evening of January 9, 1964.

A freshman at Granville High School, Danny started dating a senior girl. His parents objected, saying she was too old for him. Things came to a head when his parents demanded that Danny break off the relationship. He did not react well and by his own admission spent the next two days looking for a poison around the farm that he could use to kill his parents. Unable to find a poison, he gave up on the idea.

On Thursday, January 9, while at school, Danny and his girlfriend discussed his parents' objections and agreed to break off the relationship for a while. That evening, Danny helped with the farm chores before dinner. After dinner, Herman Leasure proceeded to the dairy barn across the street to milk the cows. Shortly after this, Danny grabbed his .22 caliber hunting rifle. He went outside, positioned himself next to a pine tree close to the kitchen window, and shot his mother in the shoulder. Stunned, she made her way to the telephone and attempted to call for help. As she picked up the receiver, Danny fired another round. Carol collapsed, dead. She was only 33 years old, having just celebrated her birthday on Christmas Day.

Danny then proceeded across the street to the dairy barn. Herman Leasure had not heard the gunshots as he had a radio on, blaring music. He had just finished preparing two cows for milking. Danny opened the barn door just wide enough to take aim. Still unnoticed by his father, he fired a round that struck Herman from the rear, killing him.

Returning to the house, Danny obtained the car keys and headed south on Burg Street toward Granville. Due to a lack of driving skills, he ran off the road into a ditch. He walked to the nearby home of Herbert Blackstone. Finding no one home, he forced his way in and called the Licking County Sheriff's Office. When the deputies arrived, they found Danny calmly sitting on the hood of the disabled car. They then went to the Leasure home, where they discovered the grisly scene. Danny's brother David soon arrived home from work and both brothers were taken into custody and lodged in the old county jail. However, David was released after authorities verified that he had been at work and had no part in the murders.

Danny initially told detectives he had been upstairs in his room when he heard shots and came downstairs to find both his mother and father dead. Mr. and Mrs. Floyd Ruffner, Danny's grandparents, were upset that they were not able to speak with their grandson, so they contacted a family friend, Don Oxley, to get advice on contacting an attorney. Mr. Oxley then called local attorney Gilbert Reese to assist the Ruffners. Reese agreed to help and made his way to the jail that night to meet with the Leasure boys.

Soon, word of the murders made its way around the community, and the high school was abuzz with rumors. Hoping to obtain an admission of guilt, officials planned to take Danny back to his home to review his story. With that, Danny agreed to confess. Reese was able to work a masterful deal for his client. He negotiated with newly appointed county prosecutor Virginia Weiss to keep the case within the juvenile system, and not try Danny as an adult. When Danny Leasure reached the age of 21 he was released from the juvenile facility. According to courthouse sources he successfully applied for a name change and left the area. Other sources indicate he went to college where he met and married a girl from a wealthy Chicago area family. Some claim they have seen Danny Leasure over the years, but none of these sightings have ever been verified. That is just one of the outstanding mysteries in this case. [34] Danny's high school girlfriend became an internationally renowned opera star, and now lives in Europe. David Leasure went to live with his grandparents and finished his senior year at Granville High School. He is now retired and lives in Texas.

The Slaying of Mary Laca

The last few months had been challenging for Howard Kibler. He was recently released from the hospital after suffering a heart attack. Back on the job as a manager at the Roper Corporation in Newark, he was trying to keep things running smoothly while several workers were out on strike. And now, well into the morning shift on

Monday, February 24, 1969, one of the secretaries, Mary Laca, had still not shown up for work. She had not called anyone to say that she would be late or needed to take a sick day. Mary was a dependable employee and not one of the workers on strike, so Kibler grew very concerned. Grabbing his coat, he rushed over to Mary's house at 552 Seroco Avenue. Soon, Kibler was confronted with something much worse than anything he had encountered before.

Mary Laca. *Courtesy of the Licking County Records and Archives Department.*

A little before 9:00 a.m., Newark policeman James Maxwell was driving along Seroco Avenue when he saw a man running towards him, waving his arms and shouting. It was Howard Kibler. Maxwell stopped his cruiser, and a distressed Kibler told him that there was a dead woman in the house at 552. Maxwell called the police station and then went up to Mary's front door, which opened into the dining room. Peering inside, he saw broken furniture and flower pots strewn across the floor. Not far away, Mary Laca was lying dead in the doorway to the kitchen. Her supper— a bowl of chili and a pot of coffee— was still on the stove. Mary herself was horribly mutilated and covered in blood. Maxwell called the station again to tell what he had found. He then made sure that the area was secure, and waited.

Mary Laca's house. *Courtesy of the Licking County Records and Archives Department.*

When Detective Chief Ned Ashton and Police Chief Charles Spurgeon entered the home they discovered, in addition to Mary Laca's mutilated, blood-covered body, a bloody sink in the bathroom, and blood splattered on the bathroom walls. A kitchen knife, its blade bent sideways at a sharp angle, was found in a drawer under the sink. Investigators also found a roll of adhesive tape, along with strips of blood stained adhesive tape, apparently from bandages. All this led them to believe this was the room where the murder was committed.

According to police, Miss Laca was murdered sometime late Saturday or early Sunday morning. She was probably stabbed about 15 times, although there was so much blood on her body that it was impossible to say for sure how many times she had been stabbed, or whether she had been beaten. She died of massive internal bleeding, and stab wounds to the heart and throughout her body. Her body had been dragged into the doorway, where blood stains marked the position in which it was found. Ned Ashton and Charles Spurgeon called the slaying "the worst thing they have seen since they have been on the police force." Her body was removed from the home over the sidewalk she used to walk to work each morning.

The day after Mary Laca's body was found, an anonymous phone call was received at the police station. The caller said that a man by the name of William Siddle had received treatment for suspicious cuts on his hands at Lancaster-Fairfield Hospital at approximately 4:55 p.m. on February 22, the suspected date of the murder. Siddle was a neighbor of Mary's who sometimes did odd jobs for her. He had been infatuated with her for roughly three years, but she had never responded to his advances. At the time, Sheriff McElroy later stated, the police were "running down anything that would be a clue to the Laca homicide." He and Detective Robert Baughman went to Siddle's residence at 24 Forry Street, less than a block from Mary's house. According to McElroy, "On arrival at the address on Forry Street, I knocked on the door, a lady answered, and I asked if Mr. Siddle was at home. The lady then turned around and said, 'Bill, there's somebody here to see you.'" McElroy said Siddle then entered the room with another man who was later identified as Harvey Holcomb. Siddle was asked to go to the station, where he was

William Siddle being escorted from his house. *Courtesy of the Newark Advocate.*

read his constitutional rights on a form, and then given a chance to read the form himself. McElroy testified that after Siddle had signed the rights form, he was fingerprinted and cuts were noticed on the fingers of his right hand. Siddle said he had received the cuts when he had been thrown from his truck in an auto accident. Prosecutor Neil Laughlin was then called to the police station. Siddle said he wanted to consult with an attorney, and was directed to a phone. "He hesitated a while in front of the phone, then broke down crying and said he needed help," McElroy noted. Siddle eventually admitted to raping and killing Mary Laca, as well as taken money from her purse.

Siddle was bound to the grand jury in a preliminary hearing held in municipal court. His attorney, Stewart Beck, called for dismissal of the case on the grounds that the state's evidence did not prove probable cause, but Judge Robert J. Moore overruled the motion, stating that "the court finds there is probable cause to send this case to the grand jury." Four witnesses took the stand for the state including George A. Gressle, coroner, and Wallace F. McElfdy, Sergeant of Detectives of the Newark Police Department.

Siddle arriving at the Licking County jail. *Courtesy of the Newark Advocate.*

During his testimony, Dr. Gressle gave a detailed account of the murder scene. He testified that Miss Laca had received multiple stab wounds to the chest that penetrated the lungs and heart. Gressle also described the nature of the cuts on Siddle's hand. When asked if it were possible to get cuts like that in an auto accident Gressle said no.

The Ohio Bureau of Criminal Identification and Investigation testified regarding their findings from the crime scene. In their investigation at Mary Laca's home, they found that Siddle's fingerprints were the same as the bloody prints found at the murder scene. A sweater, blouse, and brassiere were pushed up and over the breasts of the victim. There were many cuts in her chest area, the right side of her throat was cut, her nose appeared to be broken, her head had a number of cuts and abrasions, and her abdomen had been cut open.

Dr. George Harding and Dr. Grace Collet from the Harding Sanitarium in Worthington, Ohio examined Siddle before his trial. They testified that they found no signs of brain damage during their tests, meaning that Siddle could not be excused for his actions on the basis of insanity. Without showing any signs of remorse or guilt, Siddle told Dr. Harding, "I got a wonderful feeling when I stuck the knife in her and ripped her up."

In November 1969, after a four-week trial, Siddle was found guilty of first-degree murder and sentenced to death, although that sentence was commuted to life in prison after the Ohio Supreme Court ruled the death penalty unconstitutional. At the conclusion of the trial, Siddle was led back to the Licking County jail, and eventually transferred to the Chillicothe prison in Ross County, Ohio.

When Siddle was considered for parole on May 29, 1991, and later for a work-furlough on October 22, 1991, an outpouring of more than 800 letters from the community, as well as from a victim's rights coordinator, caused the parole board to drop consideration for his release. In 2011, when he was again up for parole, former Licking County Prosecutor Ken Oswalt wrote a letter to the parole board stating that Siddle was "incurable" and "incapable of doing anything in his 40 years of incarceration to make him an acceptable risk for release on parole." In December of 2016, Siddle became eligible for parole once more, but on January 10, 2017, the *Newark Advocate* reported that Siddle's parole was once again denied. Siddle will be eligible for another parole board hearing in December 2021, but will more than likely remain in prison for the rest of his life.

Mary Laca was a devout Christian, and was very active in her church. She was born in Newark, Ohio in 1919. She treated others with dignity and respect. She was never married, and lived alone in the home that once belonged to her parents. She didn't have many relatives in the area, but she did have a lot of good friends, friends that had a hard time understanding how such a heinous crime could happen to such a wonderful, caring person. [35]

The .22 Caliber Killers

Thaddeus and Gary Lewingdon, who became known as the ".22 Caliber Killers," or the "Blood Brothers," spread terror across three Ohio counties for an entire year. The Lewingdons went on a murderous rampage, terrorizing central Ohio with a series of fatal home invasions. The horror finally ended with their imprisonment, but not before they shattered the lives of many families. After their arrest, they had a short stay at the Licking County jail while awaiting their trial.

On December 10, 1977, Joyce Vermillion, 37, and Karen Dodrill, 33, both of Newark, were killed about 3:00 a.m. as they left Forkers Cafe in Newark, where Vermillion worked. Their frozen bodies were discovered outside the rear door of the cafe, along with several shell casings from a .22 caliber gun.

Mugshots of the Lewingdon brothers.
Courtesy of thepostmortempost.com

On February 12, 1978, Robert "Mickey" McCann, 52, his mother, Dorothy Marie McCann, 77, and McCann's girlfriend, Christine Herdman, 26, were found brutally murdered in Robert's Franklin County home. Each victim had been shot multiple times, mostly around the face and head. Shell casings from a .22 caliber gun were found scattered around the bodies.

The state Bureau of Criminal Investigation (BCI) immediately matched up the shell casings from the two shootings. "[They] told us that 'you people have got real trouble. Five people with the same gun,'" retired Newark police detective Bill Queen recalled in a 2005 interview with the *Columbus Dispatch*. "We knew then that we were dealing with a serial killer."

On April 8, 1978, Jenkin T. Jones, 77, was found dead in his Granville home from multiple gunshot wounds to his head and body. His four dogs had also been shot. Police again recovered shell casings from a .22 caliber gun. Jones was known for not trusting banks; he often told people that he would never put his money in a bank, and boasted that he kept it hidden at home instead. He apparently made this boast while purchasing some items at the Rockwell International Tool Division in Columbus, where one of the Lewingdons worked. When Jones left, his name and address were on a copy of the receipt. The next day, Gary and Thaddeus went to Mr. Jones's home. They initially fired two shots through the window of the front door, killing Jones. After ransacking the house and finding $300, they left. Later, when the authorities were conducting their investigation, they discovered $6,000 stashed in a coffee can.

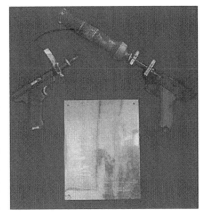

Handmade silencers used by the Lewingdons. *Courtesy of Kevin Bennett.*

On April 30, 1978, part-time security guard Rev. Gerald Fields, 35, was murdered while at work in Fairfield County. Once again, ballistic tests showed that the shell casings found at the scene matched those found at the other crime scenes.

On May 21, 1978, the Lewingdons killed their eighth and ninth victims, Jerry Martin, 47, and his wife, Martha, 51, at their Morse Road home in Franklin County. Both Jerry and Martha were shot multiple times in the head.

Home of Jenkin T. Jones. *Courtesy of Kevin Bennett.*

The final victim, Joseph Annick, 56, was killed in his eastside garage in Newark as he returned home from a friend's house about 11:30 p.m. on December 4, 1978. Seven .22 caliber shell casings were found on the floor. A credit card taken from the dead man's wallet proved to be the key to the capture of Gary and Thaddeus Lewingdon. "Thaddeus said he wasn't going to do any more murders after the Martins," Queen told the *Columbus Dispatch*. "But Gary said, 'I need money for Christmas.'"

On December 9, 1978, just one day before the anniversary of the first slaying, Cheryl Young, a 17-year-old clerk who worked at a Columbus discount store, checked the credit card that Gary Lewingdon used to buy $45 worth of toys for his children. The card, which had been Joseph Annick's, was on a list of stolen cards, and Gary Lewingdon was detained in the Great Southern Shopping Center parking lot. He confessed to being involved in the ten murders and implicated his brother in all of them except the last one.

The brothers were held in the Licking County jail until their trial. David Buxton, one of the correction officers, was in charge of guarding Thaddeus, who was kept in leg-irons as an extra precaution. Buxton described Thaddeus as keeping to himself and choosing not to speak about his crime. Both brothers were sentenced to life in prison and eventually died there. Thaddeus Lewingdon died of lung cancer on April 17, 1989, at the age of 52, while Gary died of heart failure in 2004 at the Southern Ohio Correctional Facility in Lucasville. No one, not even a family member would claim his body, so he was buried by the State of Ohio in the Mansfield prison cemetery. [36]

The John Silverwood Murder

John Silverwood was a resident of Heath, Ohio. On the evening of June 24, 1978, he encountered members of the Fugueros motorcycle gang at Dale's Bar on Wehrle Avenue in Newark. Silverwood was invited by the gang to a party that night at Clifford Bowen's property near Wilkins Corner a few miles north of Newark. At the party, Silverwood engaged in homosexual acts with at least two of the gang members. A conflict arose when he either refused to participate in these acts with a third gang member, or complained about gathering firewood. Following the argument, Silverwood was severely beaten and sexually assaulted. He was then driven to Lake Otto, near Fallsburg, where Fred Rice, the "enforcer" of the gang, beat him again and shot him to death. His body was found along the lake shore.

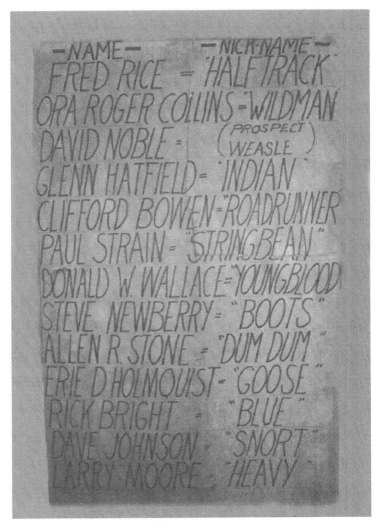

Poster found in the cell of a Fugueros gang member.

73

Three Fugueros members—Fred Rice, Ora Roger Collins, and David Noble—were convicted of murdering Silverwood. Fellow gang members Allen Stone and Eric Holmquist provided information which helped lead to the convictions, although Stone refused to testify in court after allegedly receiving threats from Rice.

In 2011, as the jail was being prepared to be opened for public tours, a poster with the names and nicknames of all the gang members was found still hanging on the wall of a second-floor cell that one of them had once occupied. This poster is currently being stored and preserved at the Licking County Records and Archives Department. [37]

George Washington Burton

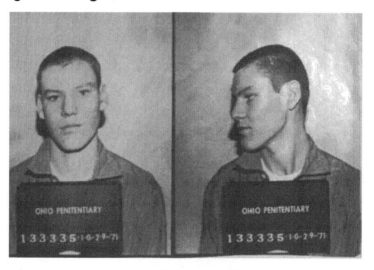

George Burton's mugshot.
Submitted Photo.

A senseless murder took place in the village of Jersey, Ohio in October, 1978. This small, peaceful village is located off of Morse Road, just a few miles southwest of Newark. The people of Jersey, once famous for its manufacturing of buggies, lived in fear until this ruthless murderer was caught.

Although it inspired great fear and is still remembered by residents of Jersey, this crime was barely mentioned in the local papers. There was no mention of it in the *Newark Advocate,* and while the *Pataskala Standard* reported on the story, much of the information provided was very limited. Most of the information about this murder was found in transcripts of the testimony given by Lt. Paul Short on November 1, 1978, detailing his investigation of this crime.

The Burton family, which included brothers George and John, lived on the north side of the village of Jersey. They had a reputation for strange behavior that made many of the neighbors afraid. Sometimes at night one of the brothers would pick up his gun and go shoot at bats. John was said to have slept in a car almost every night, even in the winter months. At times, he was seen doing other strange things. Apparently, he suffered from delusions, and it was obvious to many that he had serious mental problems.

It was not John who was the troublemaker, though. From a young age, George Burton was no stranger to crime and was often in trouble with the law. On May 26, 1971, at the age of 19, he escaped from a prison guard at the Lebanon Correctional Institution, where he was doing time for breaking and entering. His brother had died and George was escorted to the Crouse and Sons Funeral Home in Johnstown to attend the service. He managed to get away from the guard and slip out the back door of the funeral home, but was recaptured and held in the Licking County jail before being transported back to Lebanon. This was just a preview of what George Burton would do in the years to come.

In 1978, Wanda Peterman, 26, also known as Carla Andrews, lived in Jersey across the street from the Ten-Twenty Pizza and Sandwich Shop, which she ran with her husband. At least, that's what it looked like. It was later discovered that she was not married and the man she was living with may have been involved in a prostitution ring. Although this was never definitively proven, it could explain why Ms. Peterman used an alias. The authorities

Ten Twenty Pizza and Sandwich Shop. *Courtesy of the Licking County Records and Archives Department.*

speculated that this involvement might have led to the tragedy that was about to take place.

That same year, George Burton was granted parole but local authorities were not notified of his release from prison. This was a mistake that ultimately led to a terrible and senseless murder.

On October 14, 1978, George Burton went to the pizza shop where Wanda was working. When she came to the window to take his order Burton said he wanted a milkshake. After paying for it he began to walk away when he noticed that she hadn't filled his cup all the way. He returned to the window and told Wanda she had cheated him on his milkshake and he would be back with his gun.

Burton made good on his threat. He fetched his gun and returned to the shop, where he first went to the back and looked through the window. He then proceeded to walk back around to the front where Wanda was standing. Burton raised his shotgun and fired through the serving window, killing Wanda with a single blast to the chest. He then fled the scene, cutting across yards and concealing himself in the evening shadows. The owners of the shop heard the shot, saw the suspect fleeing, and ran to the pizza shop. One employee had been washing dishes in the back when she heard the shot, saw what had happened, and hid.

Body of Wanda Peterman. *Courtesy of the Licking County Records and Archives Department.*

The emergency squad from Pataskala was called, as well as the Licking and Franklin County sheriff's departments. When Burton was apprehended, he was arrested and charged with first-degree murder. He was brought to the Licking County jail where he was held until he could be transported back to the Ohio State prison, where he is today. [38]

Don't Ever Let Them out of Prison: The Roberta Peters Killing

Author's Note: the following account was written by Kevin Bennett, and is printed here with his kind permission.

In researching and writing about various murder cases, one can easily fall into the trap of being too clinical and dispassionate about these very human tragedies, especially in regards to older cases. There are cases, however, that can still arouse powerful emotional responses and outrage. The brutal killing of Roberta Ann Peters in September 1979 is one of those. It is the sad story of a young, promising life senselessly snuffed out by a couple of career criminals whose actions provide a compelling argument for the death penalty.

Roberta Peters, 23, hailed from Tucson, Arizona. A recent college graduate, she met Andrew "Andy" Merkle of Granville in

August 1979, while both were vacationing at a resort in Michigan. Deeply attracted to each other, they maintained contact and in early September, Roberta arrived in Granville. She was invited to stay at the Merkle home, in a rural area of Granville Township off State Route 16. Andy, a recent Denison University graduate soon to attend law school, lived in the country house with his mother, Margaret Merkle. In addition to continuing her romantic relationship, Roberta was actively pursuing employment in the local area as a teacher. A gifted oboe player, she also sought out association with a local symphony orchestra.

Life seemed full of promise for the couple until September 20, 1979. The day began with an air of excitement at the Merkle homestead. Margaret and a number of her family members had plans to attend the Old Brown Jug, a premier harness racing event in nearby Delaware, Ohio. The Merkle family had a long history of involvement in that sport, and the house was filled with numerous silver trophies, plates, and other racing memorabilia. Although Andy usually attended, on this occasion he declined, citing a pressing need to tend to some rental property repairs in Columbus. Roberta also demurred, indicating that she was going to help out by doing some general housecleaning at the Merkle home. Unbeknownst to them, the Merkle home had been targeted by two serial burglars, Paul Lee Duncan, 52, and Daniel Graham, 33. Graham had received a tip from an undisclosed source at the racetrack that the Merkle home would be a "big score." More importantly, the source informed him, the house was sure to be empty, as the Merkles traditionally attended the Little Brown Jug event. The information provided was detailed down to the point that Graham expressed disappointment that he would be unable to steal a valuable ring that "the old lady would probably wear to the race."

During the late morning hours, Graham and Duncan drove their cargo van down the winding Merkle driveway to the largely secluded house. Entering the home, they encountered Roberta Peters, who was busily engaged in cleaning in the kitchen area. Startled, she cried out "Who are you?" before grasping her danger. She then ran out one door chased by Paul Duncan who was armed with a .38 revolver. He quickly caught her and forcibly dragged her by the hair back inside the kitchen. Terrified, she begged for her life, but to no avail. She had seen their faces and Duncan and Graham didn't want to leave any witnesses to their crime. Duncan grabbed a small cloth from the kitchen counter, wrapped it around the muzzle of the gun, forced Peters to her knees, and fired a round into her head. The two criminals then exchanged a few sharp words, as Graham voiced his disappointment that he had not been allowed to sexually assault the girl prior to her killing. Duncan later stated that he came close to killing Graham at that time but refrained from doing so because police suspected the two worked together, and leaving Graham's body behind would probably implicate Duncan.

A bedspread from Mrs. Merkle's bedroom was used to carry Roberta's lifeless body outside. In a nearby ravine, Graham and Duncan tossed the body down into a large bramble thicket. They then commenced to loot the house, making off with over $70,000 worth of silver trophies and plates. After leaving, however, they apparently realized that the murder made the stolen goods dangerous if traced back. They drove south and threw the stolen items and the murder weapon into the Ohio River. Several days later they embarked to Portage, Michigan to burgle another location they had been tipped on.

Upon returning home around 3:30 p.m., Andy Merkle became alarmed when he noted the presence of blood in the kitchen and porch and was unable to find Peters. After a number of anguished phone calls, he searched the grounds and discovered her body. Although there was some suspicion of Duncan and Graham, police investigators came to a standstill early on and the case went unsolved.

Then, several years after the murder, there were some breaks in the case. A portion of the stolen property was discovered by two barge workers on the Ohio River. Next, two parties came forward and indicated that Duncan and Graham had told them about the burglary and murder. First, a former girlfriend of Graham, who was in custody for unrelated charges, revealed that Graham had told her his version of what had occurred during the Merkle robbery. When Paul Duncan learned that Graham had blabbed he spent months trying to track the girlfriend down so he could silence her. Accompanying him on one of these trips was a nephew who occasionally assisted in minor criminal activities. During the trip, Duncan related the story of the killing and the need to find and dispose of Graham's ex-girlfriend. Later, the nephew was arrested during the course of a burglary and came to blame Duncan for his capture, believing he had been set up. In hopes of securing a more lenient sentence he related to police the grisly tale of Paul Duncan's role in executing Roberta Peters.

By the time sufficient evidence was compiled both Duncan and Graham were already serving prison time. Both had been convicted in 1995 on federal racketeering and conspiracy charges, Duncan receiving a 40-year sentence, Graham 15 years. Finally, in 1997, they were both charged and indicted for the murder of Roberta Ann Peters. They were convicted by a Licking County jury on October 7, 1997, eighteen years, two weeks, and two days after the crime was committed. Both received a sentence of 20 years to life. Both are still incarcerated and come up for parole hearings in March 2021. Hopefully, common sense will prevail and they will remain locked away for the remainder of their miserable lives.

Prison photos of Paul Duncan (L) and Daniel Graham (R).
Courtesy of Kevin Bennett.

The Murder of Nancy Walick

Dale R. Diehl was a troubled young man. Growing up in the small, rural village of Homer, Ohio, he had a history of behavioral problems and was unable to get along with others. He was constantly in and out of trouble while attending Northridge schools, and only completed the ninth grade. He was eventually removed from his home by the juvenile court system, and placed in the Ohio Youth Commission facility. By the time he turned 18 in April of 1984, he had accumulated a juvenile record with the local courts and posed a serious threat to others.

At 18 years old, Diehl was unemployed and living at his parents' residence in Homer. On Tuesday, May 8, he drove his 1973 Chevy Vega to nearby Mt. Vernon to party with some friends, drinking beer and smoking pot. During this trip, he pulled out a .22 caliber aluminum-plated revolver he had previously stolen and offered to sell it to his friends.

Later that afternoon Diehl left the party and proceeded to a shopping mall on the east side of Mt. Vernon. He walked over to a checkout counter in the J. C. Penney store, flashed his pistol, and demanded cash from a female clerk, who gave him around $200. From there he drove to the home of a friend, Dan Huffman. That night the two partied with the money Diehl had obtained in his robbery.

The following morning Diehl drove south to the Sears store in Heath. A woman and her young daughter were out shopping for dresses and were returning to their van. After buckling her daughter in, the woman walked around to the driver's side of the van. Just as she opened the door, Diehl came up behind her, pulled back his jacket to show his pistol, and told her to get into the van. Instinctively, she hit the automatic door lock and closed the door. She told Diehl that her daughter was not feeling well, that she needed to take her to the doctor, and that he looked like a nice guy who would understand. She then said that maybe they could meet some other time.

Diehl began making remarks regarding the woman's feet and toes, and told her to take off her shoes. He then began kissing her feet and licking her toes, while keeping one hand on the pistol tucked in his waistband. Soon he began expressing his intent to engage in further sexual acts. The woman calmly stated that she did not want to perform this type of activity in public view and suggested going to the loading dock area of the Sears building. Before he could respond she began walking at a fast pace towards Sears. He tried to stop her, but she was able to reach the door first. As she entered the second door, she began screaming for help. With this, Diehl ran back to his car and drove away. This woman's clear thinking that morning undoubtedly saved her and her daughter's lives.

Apparently dissatisfied with his failure to kidnap this woman, Diehl drove to Ross's IGA grocery store just south of Granville to try again. After parking his car, he sat and watched and waited for a few minutes. At the time, a young woman by the name of Nancy Walick was in the store meeting with Gregg Ross, the owner. A sales representative, she was there to discuss merchandising cigarettes for the R.J. Reynolds Company.

Nancy had a bright future ahead of her, having recently graduated from Kent State University. She was an attractive, 23-year-old former beauty queen from Parma, Ohio, where she grew up; this was her first full-time job. Tragedy had recently struck the Walick family when Nancy's younger brother Jim accidentally drowned while on a summer church outing. Still, Nancy was moving on with her life and her parents had just helped her move into what they deemed a safe apartment complex in Columbus. On May 9, 1984, her life unfortunately intersected with Dale R. Diehl's.

Just before noon, Nancy went to the parking lot to get some promotional material from her car. As she was sorting through the material, Diehl came up behind her flashing his pistol. He ordered her into the car and told her to drive away with him.

What occurred over the next 45 minutes will never be known for sure. What is certain is that it ended with Nancy Walick dead and her body dumped on Canyon Road with a bullet wound to her head. Evidence from the police investigation revealed that she drove Diehl a few miles south of Granville to a relatively secluded rural

Body of Nancy Walick. *Submitted Photo*

area. Several vehicles passed and noted their presence. One thought they were a couple out for some necking. Another truck, driven by a local farmer, drove by around 12:15 p.m. and saw the station wagon parked alongside the road with the driver's door open. Diehl was standing outside by the door looking in. Nancy Walick was lying down on the seat with her feet towards Diehl. According to the witness, she appeared to still be alive and moving. This was the last time Nancy Walick was seen alive. About 15 minutes later another vehicle came along and observed her body sprawled on the road, her head lying in a pool of blood. She was fully clothed, but her shoes had been removed; possibly Diehl had attempted to engage in behavior similar to what he displayed with the woman at the Sears store earlier that morning.

Diehl drove Walick's car north, back toward Granville, but lost control of it on James Road after clipping a mailbox and hitting a telephone pole. Abandoning the car, he started walking, eventually hitching a ride back to a Sunoco station near the Ross's IGA store

Dale Diehl's arrest.
Courtesy of Kevin Bennett.

where he had left his car. From there he made his way to his vehicle and drove home.

Police response was rapid and investigators quickly noted the possible connection to the earlier incident at the Sears store. A massive manhunt, even utilizing helicopters, was conducted in the area surrounding the abandoned car, but with no success. When news of the murder spread, various witnesses came forward, including the two women who had given Diehl a ride to the Sunoco station. His physical description was quickly passed on to other law enforcement agencies around the state.

The next day Diehl drove to Mt. Vernon, picked up his friend Dan Huffman, and drove to Columbus. That evening they were driving south along High Street when a police cruiser noticed that Diehl's car was operating erratically. As Diehl, who had been drinking, attempted to conceal his pistol by placing it under his seat while driving, he drove up over the curb and hit a light pole. He was arrested at the scene and cited for operating a motor vehicle while intoxicated, as well as carrying a concealed weapon. His friend was released, but as it was Friday night, Diehl was held in custody over the weekend until he could be arraigned on Monday morning. A Columbus police officer, being aware of the alert, had pictures of Diehl sent over to Licking County. The pictures were shared with various witnesses and Diehl was positively identified.

Detectives from the Licking County sheriff's department went to take custody of Diehl on Monday morning, but arrived about an hour after he posted his $150 bond. His residence in Homer was immediately put under surveillance; when word arrived that he had finally returned home that night, a team of officers descended on the house. Diehl was discovered hiding in a closet and was arrested.

Meanwhile, news of the murder had been conveyed to the Walick family in Parma. As noted, they were still recovering from the recent tragic death of their son. It is difficult to conceive of the shock they must have felt. Nancy's father said the family was "completely numb." In speaking of Diehl, he could only state "He doesn't know the pain that he has caused this family." A professor at Denison University said that "everyone had the willies;" no one thought that anything like this could happen in Granville.

Diehl was indicted on charges of aggravated murder, aggravated robbery, theft of a motor vehicle, and a violation of the state firearm statute. He received a life sentence and is currently serving time in a London, Ohio prison. He will be eligible for parole in August 2033. Hopefully, when that time comes any chance for his parole will be denied and he will remain in prison for the rest of his life. [39]

Dale Diehl in prison.
Courtesy of Kevin Bennett.

Paranormal Activity at the Jail

Is the jail haunted? This is a common question and one that is asked during almost every tour of the jail. Given the dark history of the jail it certainly seems like a place that would be ripe for paranormal activity, but at the same time it is difficult for many people to believe that such activity is possible. However, teams from the United Paranormal Project have spent time at the jail and have reported several instances of possible paranormal activity. Such instances have included the sounds of footsteps, whispering voices, and flashlights turning on and off, apparently in response to questions being asked. Many of these results have been recorded on both audio and video. Ultimately, this is something that everyone has to decide for themselves; however, if you ask a member of the United Paranormal Project team, they will tell you that yes, the jail is haunted. For more information, visit their website at www.1upp.org.

Sheriffs Who Died in Office

The jail's paranormal activity isn't limited to ghostly footsteps and whisperings. Adding to the sense of possible supernatural influence is the odd string of deaths that occurred in the sheriff's quarters. During the time the jail was in operation, four sheriffs died while in office. Three of them died in the bedroom of the sheriff's residence, while the fourth had a massive heart attack in the same bedroom and died minutes later at the hospital.

Ross Embrey

The first of these sheriffs was Ross Embrey, the thirty-sixth sheriff to serve Licking County. He was elected in January 1933, and would have served through December of 1934. However, on September

Sheriff Ross Embrey. *Courtesy of the Licking County Historical Society.*

13, 1934, at just 41 years of age, he died unexpectedly of a heart attack in the residence area of the jail.

Just before retiring for the evening he had been in his office with deputies Elmer Leedy and Frank Bemar, working on official business. Mrs. Embrey stated that he walked into his room, sat down on the side of the bed, and gasped. He did not answer when she lifted his head to a pillow and spoke to him. By the time Dr. H. B. Anderson arrived, Ross Embrey was pronounced dead. It is thought that he died just after he reached the bed as he gasped for air.

Sheriff Embrey was born on March 31, 1893, near Kirkersville. He was the son of Mr. and Mrs. Thomas Embrey. He learned carpentry, and for several years was engaged in the contracting business. On June 15, 1918, he volunteered for service in World War I and served with the 209th engineers until his discharge on February 4, 1919. After his discharge, he was sent to an instructional school in the east, and later did construction work in Alabama. Upon his return to Ohio he resumed his contracting work. [40] He was also a member of the American Legion, Aladdin Shrine, and Eagle Lodge.

Sheriff Embrey entered politics in 1932, after his friends urged him to become a candidate for sheriff on the Democratic ticket. He had been in the building business most of his life, and during his term the jail was completely remodeled under his direction.

First Female Sheriff of Licking County

Less than 24 hours after the death of Sheriff Ross Embrey, Licking County commissioners held an emergency session to determine who would fill the position of sheriff until the next election. They decided upon Embrey's wife, Nora. Nora Embrey thus became the thirty-seventh sheriff, and the first woman to hold a major political office in Licking County. She was the second woman in the state of Ohio to hold the office of sheriff. The first was Anna F. Bosler of Champaign County, who became sheriff after her husband Jack was murdered. Nora filled the position until the next election in November, when Lewis D. Hague was elected. [41]

Albert Roe Francis

The second sheriff to die in office was Albert Roe Francis. He was the fortieth sheriff to serve Licking County, and was elected in January of 1947. He died suddenly at approximately 1:40 a.m. on June 12, 1949, after suffering a heart attack at the age of 59.

Albert Francis was a veteran of WWI. He served overseas for 18 months on seven fronts, and obtained the rank of sergeant. He was a member of Veterans of Foreign Wars, and the American Legion.

Mrs. Francis was the jail's cook and prepared meals for both the prisoners and her family. She wanted to be appointed to take over for her husband, which would have made her the second woman to become sheriff of Licking County. However, the commissioners decided to appoint former Sheriff William McElroy instead.

Sheriff Francis and his wife are buried at Cedar Hill Cemetery in Newark, Ohio. [42]

Sheriff Albert Roe Francis. *Courtesy of the Licking County Historical Society.*

Sheriff William McElroy. *Courtesy of the Licking County Historical Society.*

William McElroy

On March 23, 1962, Licking County residents mourned the death of yet another sheriff when William McElroy became the third victim of a heart attack while serving in office. He, too, died in the bedroom of the sheriff's living quarters.

McElroy was 59 years old and had a history of heart ailments. He and his wife Helen had just returned from Columbus where they had been visiting and shopping. They had also finished transporting two convicted felons, Calvert V. Racey and Raymond E. Smith, to the Ohio Penitentiary to start serving prison sentences.

After returning from Columbus around 5:45 p.m., McElroy went to his bedroom to change his clothes. A few minutes later Mrs. McElroy went to the bedroom and found the sheriff lying on the bed, dead. He was officially pronounced dead upon the arrival of the family physician.

McElroy was known throughout the state as a top law enforcement officer and had received many awards during the previous twenty years.

On April 11, 1942, he had a narrow brush with death when his car skidded out of control on an icy patch on Route 40 near Kirkersville and slid into a creek. He was thrown from the car and lay there for two hours, exposed to the rain and snow, before being found. He received a fractured hip from the accident, which caused him to limp the rest of his life.

McElroy had already served one term as sheriff before being reappointed after the death of Albert Francis, making him both the thirty-ninth and the forty-first sheriff of Licking County. [43]

Bernard Howarth

On October 4, 1971, Sheriff Bernard Howarth, age 58, became the fourth sheriff to die in office. The forty-third sheriff of Licking County, Howarth also suffered a massive heart attack while in the sheriff's residence of the jail. He died just a few minutes after arriving at the hospital. About one week earlier he had been released from the hospital after spending two months in the coronary care unit.

Howarth was born on March 4, 1913. He was serving his second term as sheriff, an office he was elected to in 1964. He began his law enforcement career as an Ohio Highway Patrol Trooper from 1938 to 1944. He spent 16 years as a member of the Newark police department, retiring with the rank of captain. When he was elected sheriff, he was the first person in the county who had served with all three types of law enforcement.

Following Sheriff Howarth's death, Newark Mayor James Alexander ordered the city's flags lowered to half-mast. On October 4, 1971, Sheriff Howard's wife, Christine Graybill Howarth, was appointed to become Licking County's forty-fourth sheriff. She

Sheriff Bernard Howarth.
Courtesy of the Licking County Historical Society.

completed her husband's term, ending in November of 1972. Bernard Howarth was buried at Cedar Hill Cemetery in Newark.

After three sheriffs died in the same bedroom, and the fourth suffered a massive heart attack while in the sheriff's residence, one might begin to ask: could this just be a series of unfortunate coincidences? Or is there something more going on, perhaps something beyond the realm of human understanding? [44]

Anonymous Interviews

The following information was learned from an anonymous interview with an inmate who spent time in the Licking County jail in 1976. His cell was the third cell on the north side of the corridor on the second floor. He did not want to share the reason why he ended up in jail, but he did tell me it wasn't a violent crime. This led me to believe that he might have been charged with drunk and disorderly conduct. Much of what he was willing to share was not only interesting, but also demonstrated the ingenuity of these men. He and three other inmates managed to escape from their second-floor cells, but were caught two days later. As a result, they served additional time for their effort.

He described how inmates would heat up their leftover coffee by splitting a razor blade in half, attaching the two pieces to an electric cord, placing it in their coffee, and plugging it in. Although this was not a very safe practice, it was effective.

He said there was a pipe that passed through all four floors of the jail. The pipe was eventually removed, but the portion that runs through the floor remains. This was used by the inmates to pass cigarettes and notes from floor to floor. It wasn't uncommon for some inmates to roll their own cigarettes. The Bugler brand paper was a common brand used to roll tobacco. Many unused gummed cigarette papers, like the one shown at the right, were found stuck under the bunks and along the wall in some of the cells.

This inmate also described how he lost a finger when his cell door was slammed on his hand. It seems that it was common practice for inmates to try to keep their door from latching by stuffing paper in the lock as it was being closed. Although he didn't say this was what he was trying to do, it may have been the reason why his finger got caught in the door. He said the time he spent in this jail was probably

Bugler Brand cigarette wrapping paper.

the worst time of his life, but he did admit to being a rowdy teenager, which may have contributed to getting started off on the wrong foot early in his life.

Anonymous Interview, 2012

In 1978 a female inmate, who was just 18 at the time, was arrested for shoplifting with her young daughter. She spent two months in the Licking County jail for her crime. She said the time she spent in jail taught her a very valuable lesson and helped her turn her life around. Her cell on the fourth floor was next to a very loud and obnoxious woman who was arrested for a more serious crime, but in spite of their differences they managed to get along.

Inmates were not supposed to get loud and talk to each other, but most did whenever they could. Sometimes, when they had access to the windows facing the parking lot on the south side, they would yell through the barred opening to pedestrians below, to try to strike up a conversation. This would only continue as long as the Matron didn't hear them; if she did she would immediately close the narrow steel doors covering the barred opening, to prevent them from even looking outside.

One of the women discovered a small crack through the floor at the end of the corridor that led to the male prisoners below. Sometimes, the women were able to look through this crack and see the male inmates below. They were even able to communicate with them by dropping a note through the crack on a string. For the most part the women were well behaved and did not cause much trouble. The interviewed inmate said "I guess this was why, on occasions, the Matron would buy a pizza for us, and tell everyone not to say anything, as the only food we were supposed to receive was what was supplied by the jail." [45]

Closing of the Jail

In 1978 new state standards for places of incarceration were adopted. The standards adopted locally became effective on September 5, 1978. The Licking County jail did not meet the minimum standards in many different categories. These new standards spelled out everything from operations of the jail to how much room a prisoner must have. The inmate population would now be reduced to a maximum of two prisoners per cell instead of four, and emergency medical treatment must now be available on a 24-hour basis. Making recreation available would also become a requirement, and safety concerns had to be addressed. Because the jail could not meet most of the new standards and the county wanted to avoid the possibility of a lawsuit, it was closed in 1987 and replaced with a more modern facility. [46]

For several years, the jail became a storage facility for many of Licking County's records. The jail cells were filled with hundreds of boxes of records containing everything from traffic violations to mortgage deeds, probate records, and much more. Through an extensive effort, and at the direction and recommendation of the county commissioners, plans were made to move valuable documents to the Licking County Records & Archives building, where they could be properly maintained and stored in a controlled environment, and shred those documents deemed to be unnecessary, or that no longer served any useful purpose.

Fortunately, the county took a proactive view and plans were made to restore the historic jail and open it to the public for tours. For many years, this beautifully designed building, long admired from the outside, sat here waiting to be discovered and admired from the inside as well. Its day has finally come, and through the efforts of the county commissioners, the staff at the Licking County Records

& Archives Department, and many volunteers, this amazing historic jail can now be seen and appreciated by the general public.

It has become a tourist attraction in its own right. A tour of the jail will give you the feeling that you have stepped back in time as you get a glimpse into the past. You can only imagine what it must have been like to live during the early 1900s. For many who chose to break the law, it no doubt became a daily struggle to endure the time they served in this jail. The harsh conditions they lived in doubtless served as a constant reminder that this was not a hotel, and they were here for a reason.

You did not necessarily have to commit a crime in the 1900s to be imprisoned. In the early 1900s, the sheriff was responsible for the confinement of afflicted people, as well as criminals. If someone acted strange— or at least, in a way that seemed strange to others— you could file a complaint with the sheriff. Your complaint would then be reviewed by the sheriff, or sometimes by a physician. If it was deemed necessary, the sheriff would transport that person to a state mental institution. The Licking County Lunacy Records have actual cases of people who were committed to a mental hospital for virtually no reason at all.

According to legend, in one case a 56-year-old woman was committed to the Athens State Mental Hospital because "she had fits due to the change of life." In another case, a 22-year-old man was committed to the state mental hospital because "he couldn't adjust to married life." Thank goodness those days are behind us, but it is interesting to look back at old records like these and get a glimpse into what life must have been like at that time. [47]

The Licking County Records and Archive Department stores and maintains thousands of county records, preserving them in a controlled environment. They have the tedious and time-consuming task of entering historical document information on the county's website to aid the public in their research of Licking County history. Many documents are also being recorded on microfilm to electronically preserve much of Licking County's history.

Cleaning, documenting, and storing these records is a monumental task, and one that is necessary to preserve the county's history. The preservation of Licking County's history is important for future generations.

To research Licking County history, visit their website at: www.lcounty.com.

Other Jails of Licking County

The first Licking County jail was built on the courthouse square in 1808, the same year the county was founded. A simple, two-story log cabin structure, it burned to the ground in 1815, along with the original courthouse.

The second jail was built in 1815 in the rear of the Park House Hotel, on East Main St. A Wendy's restaurant is located there now.

A third jail was built in 1840 on the south side of the canal between First and Second street. It was condemned in 1887 due to multiple safety concerns, and the Licking County Historic Jail was built to replace it.

The current jail, or Justice Center, as it is called, was built to replace the Historic Jail when it was closed in 1987. It is located on East Main Street, just east of the Licking County Courthouse, near downtown Newark.

Sheriffs of Licking County

John Stadden Elected in 1808

Andrew Baird Elected in 1810

Andrew Allison Elected in 1814

John Cunningham 1818 – 1822

William W. Gault 1822 – 1822

Elias Howell 1826 – 1830

William Spencer 1830 – 1834

Richard Stradden 1834 – 1838

William P. Morrison 1838 – 1840

Caleb Boring 1840 – 1844

William Veach 1844 – 1848

William Parr 1848 – 1852

William A. Bell Jr. 1852 – 1854

Hiram Tenney 1854 – 1859

William A. Bell Jr. 1859 – 1863

Jonathan E. Rankin 1863 –1867

Jeremiah Siler 1867 – 1871

Edwin Williams 1871 – 1875

Samuel H. Schofield 1875 – 1979

Allen T. Howland 1879 – 1883

George W. Hall 1883 – 1887

James Madison Browne Jr. 1887 –

Andrew Crilly 1887 – 1891 (first sheriff to live in the jail)

Rowlison P. Ford 1891 – 1895

John A. Chilcott 1895 – 1897

George William Horton 1897 – 1901

William Hobart Anderson 1901 – 1904

Smith L. Redman 1904 –

William Linke 1909 – 1910 (relieved of his duties after the lynching of Carl Etherington)

Frank Slabaugh 1910

Charles H. Swank 1915 – 1919

Elijah A. Bryan 1919 – 1923

Fredrick Henry Vogelmeier 1923 – 1926

Carl Ray Foulk 1927 – 1928

Festus T. Hoover 1929 – 1932

Ross A. Embrey 1933 – 1934 (died while serving in office)

Nora Embrey 1934 (appointed to finish her husband's term)

Lewis Dayton Hague 1934 – 1941

William A. McElroy 1941 –

Albert Roe Francis 1947 – 1949 (died while serving in office)

William McElroy 1949 – (died while serving in office)

John F. Koontz Sr. 1962 – 1964

William Bernard Howarth 1965 – (died while serving in office)

Christine Graybill Howarth 1971 – 1973

Max B. Marston 1973 –

Gerry D. Billy 1981 – 2004

Randy Thorp 2005

Notes

The black iron fence in front of the jail was installed in 1889 by Lane Brothers, after the jail was completed. The total cost of the fence was $750, including labor and materials. Reference page 278 in the Commissioner's Journal, book #6, located in the Licking County Administration Building on the 4th floor.

The old jail lot was sold at auction for $3,300 in December 1889.

Reference page 296 of commissioner's journal book #6, located in the Licking County Administration Building on the fourth floor.

References

1 *Newark Daily Advocate,* June 14, 1888 pg. 4

2 Commissioner's Journal, No. 6 page 128 September 15, 1888

3 Commissioner's Journal, No. 6 May 7, 1889 page 203

4 *Newark Weekly Advocate,* May 15, 1889, pg. 4 Ohio

5 *Newark American,* December 19, 1889

6 *Newark Weekly Advocate,* November 26, 1889 pg.4 Ohio Historical Society Microfilm Roll #7 the Licking County Library

7 *Newark American,* December 5, 1889 Ohio Historical Society pg. 8

8a Information about overcrowding provided by retired Licking County Sheriff Gerry D. Billy

8b Board of Licking County Visitors September 20, 1917, Records & Archives Dept. (Location 9A21)

9 *Newark Daily Advocate,* September 16, 1895

10 *Newark Daily Advocate,* Wednesday February 26, 1896 pg. 5

11 *Semi Weekly Advocate,* September 24, page 1, 1907

12 *Cleveland Plain Dealer,* July 9, 1910 pg 1, Newark Advocate's 100 anniversary of this event was documented in great detail, July 11, 2010 pg 1. additional information about convictions was verified from Licking County court records.

13 *Newark Advocate,* October 23, 1935 page 1 & follow up stories from December 2 – 6, pages 1-2, and the Columbus Dispatch Sunday Star, October 11, 1936 pages 18, 19, 34

14 *Newark Daily Advocate,* Wednesday April 27, 1904

15 *Newark Daily Advocate,* June 13, 1905 pg. 8

16 *Newark Advocate,* June 17, 1905 pg 4

17 *Newark Advocate,* June 4, 1916

18 *Newark Advocate,* August 12, 1930 pg 1

19 *Newark Advocate,* July 14, 1953
20 *Newark Advocate,* September 22, 1961
21 *Newark Advocate,* March 10, 1962.
22 *Newark Advocate,* Thursday December 18, 1975 pg. 3
23 *Newark Advocate,* Friday May 30, 1975
24 Reference the *Newark Advocate,* Monday, June 13, 1978 Ohio Historical Society Licking County Library.
25 *Newark Advocate,* June 2, and June 10, 1905
26 *Mansfield News,* March 31, 1911
27 *Newark Advocate,* July 2, 1931; Newark Advocate, October 15, 1938.
28 *Newark Advocate,* October 15, 1938
29 *Newark Advocate,* November 4, 1938
30 *Newark Advocate,* January 6, 1947 pg 1 and pg 2 column 1
31 *Newark Advocate,* September 15, 1951 pg 1 & pg 2 col 4
32 *Newark Advocate,* March 17, 1952 pg 1
33 *Newark Advocate,* September 17, 1956 pg.1 & 2
34 *Newark Advocate,* January 9, 2014, (50 year anniversary recap of this tragedy.) Researched and written by Kevin Bennett, local historian.
35 *Newark Advocate,* February 25 1969, pg. 1 and pg.10 pg.1 By Dave Graff and the Newark Advocate, Wednesday, March 19, 1969. Excerpts from Licking County Prosecutor and examining doctor.
36 *Newark Advocate,* Cincinnati Post, Columbus Dispatch, Charles Montaldo crime investigator.
37 *Newark Advocate,* 1978.Information provided by Bill Markley, Licking County Records & Archives.
38 *Pataskala Standard,* October 18, 1978 pg 1.
39 *Granville Sentinel,* August 9, 1984 submitted by Kevin Bennett.
40 *Newark Advocate,* September 14, 1934 pg 1
41 From Bicentennial Highlight No. 5 by Dan Fleming, Submitted to the Newark Advocate February 28, 2008
42 *Newark Advocate,* June 12, 1949

43 Newark Advocate, March, 24, 1962
44 Newark Advocate, October 5, 1971
45 Anonymous interviews provided by local people who served time for minor offences
46 Newark Advocate, January 31, 1979.
47 Referenced from the Licking County Lunacy Records, located at the Licking County Records and Archive Department

About the Author

 Neil Phelps became interested in writing about Licking County's historic jail while he was a volunteer for the Licking County Records and Archive Department in 2010. It was here that he helped with the restoration of old county records, including many jail registers from the 1800s.

Working under the supervision of Records Clerk Bill Markley, he helped identify hundreds of boxes of county records from various agencies that had been stored at the jail for over two decades.

His background is primarily in electronics, having graduated from DeVry Technical Institute in Chicago, and worked as a civilian employee for the Government. He was later employed with the Boeing Corporation, where he was in charge of maintaining software for the Minute Man and PeaceKeeper defense programs.

After working with the Licking County Records and Archives Department for two years, he became more involved in local history, and focused most of his research on the Historic Licking County Jail. He joined the Licking County Historical Society and was appointed to serve as a trustee. He also serves on the Events Committee, and the Research and Archival Committee for the jail, and helps with tours of the jail during the summer months. He is a member of the Newark/Granville Toastmasters Club, and has given presentations about the history of the jail and its inmates at club meetings.